PLAY and LEARN
French

Second Edition

Ana Lomba *and* Marcela Summerville

Illustrations by Pedro Pérez del Solar and Corne Cartoons/Enroc Illustrators

French Translation by Gaëlle Goutain

New York   Chicago   San Francisco   Lisbon   London   Madrid   Mexico City
Milan   New Delhi   San Juan   Seoul   Singapore   Sydney   Toronto

The **McGraw·Hill** Companies

1 2 3 4 5 6 7 8 9 10 11 12 13 14 15   CTP/CTP   1 9 8 7 6 5 4 3 2 1

ISBN   978-0-07-175924-3 (book and CD set)
MHID   0-07-175924-7 (book and CD set)

ISBN   978-0-07-175922-9 (book for set)
MHID   0-07-175922-0 (book for set)

e-ISBN   978-0-07-178168-8
e-MHID   0-07-178168-4

Library of Congress Control Number   2011929607

Interior artwork copyright © by Pedro Pérez del Solar and Corne Cartoons/Enroc Illustrators
Interior design by Think Design Group LLC

McGraw-Hill books are available at special quantity discounts to use as premiums and sales promotions or for use in corporate training programs. To contact a representative, please e-mail us at bulksales@mcgraw-hill.com.

This book is printed on acid-free paper.

Contents

Acknowledgments

We would like to express our heartfelt thanks and appreciation to the many friends and colleagues who have encouraged and supported us along the way.

A special thanks is due to the following people, who have facilitated book production and design:

- Pedro Pérez del Solar, illustrator, for his magical ability to bring our stories to life

- Corne Cartoons/Enroc Illustrators for the wonderful new illustratons in this second edition

- Corinne Güngör, founder and director of the French School of Princeton, for the French translation of the first edition

- Gaëlle Goutain, education director of L'Alliance Française of Princeton, for the translation of the new content in this edition and for many other projects. Thanks so much!

- Rob Zollman, musician, for the recordings of the first edition, and for all the fun we had making them!

- Bonnie Blader, Ana's dear friend and unofficial proofreader, for her golden touch with language, adding flair to the English translation

- Karen Young, our editor at McGraw-Hill, who guided us through the process of writing this book with keen insight and friendly advice.

We would also like to thank all those people in our personal lives who have made this book possible:

- Joseph, Victoria, Ana, Tyler, and Marina, our children, who are our constant inspiration

- Ozzie and John, our husbands, for their eternal patience—we couldn't have done it without you!

- Our readers and students, for being our best fans

This book is dedicated to Ana's beloved daughter, Marina, a special-needs child who reminds us every day of the miracle of learning.

Introduction

Young children are to language what ducklings are to water. Let them jump in and play!

—Ana Lomba

Welcome to a new edition of *Play and Learn French*! It is because of forward thinking and visionary parents, grandparents, and educators like you that tens of thousands of children are now using *Play and Learn* to learn French in early childhood—*the prime time for language learning*. Bravo!

You sent us e-mails, posted comments on our blogs, talked to us via social media, and we listened! As you will soon discover, we have included many of your great suggestions in this book.

In this new edition you will be able to:

- Listen to the picture vocabulary words and strips on each page.

- Focus on a scene at a time (no need to listen to the entire theme anymore!).

- Enjoy listening to professional voice-over talents (Marcela and I did our best, but we are certainly not voice professionals!).

In addition, not only will you learn new vocabulary through five new themes, but you will also:

- Learn how to scaffold language by playing two board games in French.

- Learn how to teach like a pro with the strategies included in this introduction.

Ana Lomba's Easy Immersion® Method

There is plenty of research today showing that early childhood is the prime time for learning languages. We also know that young children learn languages best in interactive exchanges with their parents or teachers.

Unfortunately, over the last few years there has been a spike of flashcard-based foreign language programs especially targeted to young children. While your child may learn a few words and phrases from these programs, this type of approach is quite detrimental in the long run, as precious time is wasted on activities that do not lead to authentic real-life proficiency. Your child will learn much more in the context of playing and speaking with you!

Ana's breakthrough method ("Ana Lomba's Easy Immersion®") is based on three principles:

- Young children learn a new language best when they use it in everyday situations.

- Young children learn a new language best when they use it to interact with their parents, teachers, and friends.

- Young children learn a new language best when there is a bridge between the home and the school.

A large majority of the adults teaching French or other languages to young children are not native speakers and do not hold degrees in language education (much less in early language education). This, however, should not be seen as an impediment to teaching languages. Moreover, it should not be seen as an impediment to teaching in an immersive way.

The fact that you are not fluent in French or that you are a total beginner in French does not mean that you can only teach words to your kids. It just means that you will need more support in order to do that. This is where Ana's Easy Immersion comes to the rescue. Ana's materials provide content and how-to knowledge for non-native and native parents and teachers who want to teach languages in a way that targets real-life proficiency.

Play and Learn French and Ana's other materials are designed to assist parents and teachers who:

- Are serious about learning French with their children.

- Look forward to the challenge and the rewards of learning a new language.

- Believe that they can be the initial motor that sparks their children's world language education.

The word "Easy" before "Immersion" does not mean that learning French will always be easy. Instead, it is used to make a distinction between your experience using Ana's method from that of landing in a foreign country not speaking a word of the language—that would certainly be hard! As you will discover with *Play and Learn French*, you will immediately understand the content and be able to use it with your children.

One final thought on Ana's Easy Immersion: when you start using this book, you may think that the recorded speakers talk too fast. This is to be expected! You are immersing yourself in authentic speech, after all. Give it time for the language to sink in and become your own. This is no different from listening to a song for the first time and trying to remember all the lyrics. Each time you will understand more, and soon enough you will be able to use the new language even in spontaneous conversations.

How to Use This Book

Start with the activities most interesting to your child. This program isn't based on a linear progression. Begin with the activity you think your child will enjoy and proceed as you wish. Some situations are easier and others more complicated; thus the activities and conversations accommodate different ages and language levels.

Use the illustrations as a picture dictionary. Visual input will help strengthen understanding, accelerate oral fluency, and facilitate emerging literacy in the new language. Read the captions at the bottoms of the pages while pointing to the pictures, and then ask your child simple questions like *Laquelle est la fourchette?* (Which one is the fork?), *Où est le train?* (Where is the train?), or *Qu'est-ce que c'est?* (What is this?). Key French words and expressions (and their English counterparts) in the activities, games, and songs are **boldfaced** to facilitate learning and help build new vocabulary.

Children's lines in song lyrics and responses in activities appear in *italics*.

Take it easy. We recommend taking baby steps. Don't try to learn everything at once. Follow your own child's learning rhythm. Start with the expressions or vocabulary words that you think will be most appealing to your child and then build by using the expressions in other situations as well.

Use the new language frequently. Set your own goals and work at your own pace. Your child will benefit from as little as fifteen minutes of French three to four times a week. Please try to make these moments feel as natural and playful as possible and always follow your child's lead.

Don't let pronunciation stop you. Traditional language learning programs put too much emphasis on pronunciation, which has proven counterproductive again and again. Your pronunciation will improve as you go. Our goal is to help you to communicate with all French speakers, not to speak with a perfect French accent. Your children will have an advantage over you in pronunciation, as their young minds will be able to register sounds to which you may have become deaf.

Make it a game. Your attitude is important. Young children respond better to exciting and playful endeavors than to formal "sit-and-recite" learning. Make learning French a game.

Don't hesitate to use the new language in front of French speakers. Why are you learning French if not to speak with native speakers? Chances are you and your child will make new friends and will enrich your knowledge of the new language and culture.

Expand the learning experience. Consider creating a language corner for your child. The corner can include books, postcards, posters, and other culture-oriented items. If you have friends traveling to another country, ask them to bring you postcards, subway maps, menus, and other small souvenirs. Encourage your child to "teach" French to other family members. In this way you can build beyond the exercises in this book.

Focus on your interaction with your child. The best way to learn a language is through personal interaction. Tapes, videos, and other materials will help, but they will never be enough. That is why we encourage you to speak to your child in French. Never assume your child will effectively learn by simply parroting a tape or video.

Use the language naturally. Avoid constant translation and unnecessary explanations. If you translate to children, they will not make the effort to learn the new language. Use translation only if you see your child becoming frustrated.

Encourage but don't force speaking. Most children immersed in a second language pass through an initial "silent" period. While called "silent," it is not necessarily so, as children may respond in their first language. This is fine. Children need time to figure out the links between the new words and concepts, to understand, as well as to register and practice new sounds.

Don't be overly concerned about language "confusion." Mixing words, accents, and even grammatical structures is normal among young bilinguals. Contrary to common belief, this is not necessarily a sign of language confusion or of speech or language delay. Unfortunately, this common misunderstanding about language learning is the cause of much unnecessary sacrifice and suffering for families who are advised to drop the second language. If you are concerned about your bilingual child's language development, seek the help of a therapist who specializes in bilingual issues, and educate yourself on the topic as well.

About the Language Used in This Book

One-on-one relationships. Our program focuses on one-on-one interaction to simplify learning and better respond to parental needs. While you will not learn plural verb forms at this point, learning them will be much easier and less confusing in the future. These activities can easily be adapted to teach a larger group of children by simply using the plural forms of the verbs.

One-way exchanges. In most situations, the parent is the only speaker. This is because children need a lot of input before they are able to speak, just as happens when parents speak to their children in their first language. Children begin producing utterances when they feel ready after hearing modeled speech.

Gender. In French, all nouns are either masculine or feminine. Because articles must agree in gender and number (i.e., singular or plural) with the noun they modify, it is a good idea to look at the article to determine if the noun is feminine or masculine. The masculine singular articles are "le" and "un" (*le*

garçon = the boy; *un garçon* = a boy). The feminine singular articles are "la" and "une" (*la fille* = the girl; *une fille* = a girl). "L' " is used when the first letter of the word is a vowel or, sometimes, an "h" (*l'eau* = the water; *l'hôpital* = the hospital). "Du" or "de la" can also be used with singular nouns to indicate "some" (*du lait* = some milk; *de la salade* = some salad; *de l'eau* = some water). "Les" or "des" are used with plural nouns (*les fleurs* = the flowers; *des fleurs* = some flowers). Sometimes the articles "du," "de la," or "des" can indicate a general, all-encompassing meaning (*les bébés boivent du lait* = babies drink milk). Like articles, adjectives change gender and number as well. We have indicated differences in gender with slashes in the text (*belle/beau* = pretty/handsome).

"Teach-Like-a-Pro" Strategies for Teachers

While this book was initially created for parents, many teachers are using it as well. We appreciate our colleagues' trust and support, and we offer these strategies as our way to say, "thank you"! We hope you find them helpful!

• **Work on a theme, not on isolated activities.** For example, you could create a unit based on the theme of "Winter and Health." Young children tend to get sick a few times during the winter season, and this is a great opportunity to talk about germs, going to the doctor, washing hands, and many other topics related to the winter and health. Select scenes from the book connected to the theme.

• **Extend the theme and integrate subjects.** If you talk about Bastille Day for a week and the next week about polar bears, your students will have a very hard time learning French. They may remember a word here and there, but that's all. Instead, extend the topic for a few weeks and integrate content from other area subjects. For example, in a "Winter and Health" unit, they could learn numbers to take their friends' temperature (math and science), draw a snowman (art), and learn the names and functions for some parts of the body (science).

• **Work on all four language skills but focus on speaking.** Integrating listening, speaking, reading, and writing from the very beginning is the magic key to take you further sooner. For very young children, "reading" may mean that *you* read a story to them or that they pretend to read a book that they have memorized in French. Writing may mean practicing small motor skills and scribbling. Older students could listen to the situations in this book (without reading) and try to figure out what is happening. Note, however, that nothing will motivate your students more than being able to speak, so make a point of practicing speaking every day. At the beginning, you could just ask them to repeat after you. To encourage independent speaking, ask frequent questions, especially of the "w" and "h" type (when, why, where, who, which, and how). Do all of this in French, of course!

• **Establish a school-home connection.** Recommend resources such as *Play and Learn French* and Ana's other materials to your students' families and encourage them to learn French with their children. *No other formula is more powerful in early language education than the collaboration between teachers and parents.* That is why Ana's materials have been designed for use in school and at home.

We love hearing from families and teachers. If you are using *Play and Learn French* let us know how you do!

Bonjour

Good

[handwritten note: est = a]

[handwritten note: SAturda / SA laya]

C'est l'heure de se lever!

Bonjour! C'est l'heure de se lever!
Réveille-toi, mon chéri. **Le soleil**
  est levé.
C'est l'heure de se lever! Bonjour!
Oh, comme tu as sommeil!
Réveille-toi, mon chéri.
Regarde, il fait jour. Le soleil est levé.
Soleil, petit soleil, réchauffe-moi,
Aujourd'hui et demain et toute
  la semaine.
Debout, paresseux!
Donne-moi ta main.
Oh, comme tu as sommeil!
Allez, on y va.
Fais attention aux **marches**.
Doucement. C'est ça.
Allons à **la cuisine**.
Qu'est-ce que tu aimerais pour ton
  petit déjeuner?

Time to Get Up!

Good morning! It's time to get up!
Wake up, honey. The **sun**
  is out.
It's time to get up! Good morning!
Oh, **how sleepy**!
Wake up, honey.
Look, it's daytime. The sun is out.
Sun, little sun, warm me up,
Today and tomorrow and all
  week long.
Up, lazy one!
Give me your hand.
Oh, how sleepy!
Come on, let's go.
Be careful with the **steps**.
Slowly. That's it.
Let's go to the **kitchen**.
What would you like for
  breakfast?

Did You Know?

In French, an adjective agrees in number and gender with the noun it describes.
For example: un sac vert (masculine singular) becomes des sacs verts
(masculine plural). Un navire bleu (masculine singular), but une valise bleue
(feminine singular) and des valises bleues (feminine plural). The adding
of an "e" to the end of an adjective generally indicates the feminine gender,
and adding an "s" indicates the plural form, although there are exceptions.

[handwritten note: ER - verb TO DO something]

[handwritten note: Don't pronounce S unless e at end]

...me tu as som...

La cuisine

8

C'est l'heure du petit déjeuner!

Time for Breakfast!

C'est l'heure du petit déjeuner.	It's time to have breakfast.
Aide-moi. Mettons la table.	Help me. Let's set the table.
Voilà **les céréales**. *Miam!*	Here is the **cereal**. *Yum!*
Voilà **le lait**.	Here is the **milk**.
Que nous faut-il d'autre?	What else do we need?
*Il faut **du jus d'orange**.*	*We need **orange juice**.*
Veux-tu du jus d'orange?	Do you want orange juice?
Voilà **les bols de céréales**.	Here are the **cereal bowls**.
Que nous faut-il d'autre?	What else do we need?
*Il nous faut **des cuillères**.*	*We need **spoons**.*
Que faut-il d'autre?	What else do we need?
*Il faut **des verres** pour le jus.*	*We need **glasses** for the juice.*
Voilà les verres pour le jus.	Here are glasses for the juice.
Lequel veux-tu, le vert ou le jaune?	Which one do you want, the green one or the yellow one?
Le vert.	*The green one.*
Très bien. Tout est prêt.	All right. Everything is ready.
Assieds-toi pour manger ton petit déjeuner.	Sit down to eat breakfast.
Oh, non! Tu as renversé le jus.	Oh, no! You spilled the juice.
Tiens, nettoie toi-même.	Here, clean yourself.

Le lait

Le bol

La cuillère

Le verre

Comme tu es belle/beau!

Avec de l'eau très propre,
*Mon **visage** je vais laver.*
Avec du dentifrice et une brosse à dents,
mes dents je vais laver.
Mets **le dentifrice** sur **la brosse**.
Brosse tes dents.
Lalalalalalalalalala.
*Maintenant avec **le peigne**,*
*Je vais peigner mes **cheveux**.*
*Je me regarde dans **le miroir**.*
Ouah! Je vais être si belle/beau!
Ouah! Comme tu es belle/beau!

You Look So Beautiful/ Handsome!

With very clean water,
*my **face** I will wash.*
With toothpaste and a toothbrush,
my teeth I will brush.
Put the **toothpaste** on the **toothbrush**.
Brush your teeth.
Chachachachachacha.
*Now with the **comb**,*
*I will comb my **hair**.*
*I look at myself in the **mirror**.*
Wow! I will look so pretty/handsome!
Wow! How pretty/handsome you look!

Did You Know?

Constantly correcting a person's language does not help in the language learning process. In fact, it actually interferes with it. A better way to help is to model. For example, if your child says, "Je suis froid" (using the verb être/to be *when the expression requires the verb* avoir/to have*), just smile and say, "As-tu froid? Moi aussi, j'ai froid."*

Le dentifrice

La brosse à dents

Le peigne

Le miroir

C'est l'heure de s'habiller!

Time to Get Dressed!

C'est l'heure de s'habiller!
Regardons dans l'armoire.
Voyons—**des pantalons, des jupes,**
Des chemisiers, des t-shirts...
Qu'est-ce que tu veux mettre?
Veux-tu la jupe rouge?
Ce pantalon?
Ce t-shirt vert
ou le chemisier jaune?
Le jaune.
Très bien. Enfile **un bras**.
Enfile l'autre bras.
Passe **la tête**. Ça y est!
Et quoi d'autre? Ce **short**?
Bien. Tiens-toi à moi.
Enfile **une jambe**.
Enfile l'autre jambe.
Ça y est!
Ouah, comme tu es jolie!

Time to get dressed!
Let's look in the closet.
Let's see—**pants, skirts,**
shirts, T-shirts . . .
What do you want to put on?
Do you want the red skirt?
These pants?
The green T-shirt
or the yellow shirt?
The yellow one.
Very good. Put in your **arm**.
Put in your other arm.
Put in your **head**. All done!
And what else? The **shorts**?
Good. Hold on to me.
Put in your **leg**.
Put in your other leg.
All done!
Wow, how nice you look!

Un pantalon

Une jupe

Un t-shirt

Un short

Allons dehors!
Let's Go Outside!

Il fait froid!
Il fait chaud!

It's Cold! It's Hot!

Voyons quel temps il fait aujourd'hui.
Ah! Il fait si froid! Comme il fait froid!
Il fait très froid! Il fait très froid!
Je mets mon **chandail** car il fait
    très froid.
Il fait très froid! Il fait très froid!
Je mets mon **bonnet** car il fait
    très froid.
Il fait très froid! Il fait très froid!
Je mets ma **veste**.
Je mets mes **gants**.
Je mets mon **écharpe**.

Rentrons maintenant. Ah!
    Il fait très chaud!
Il fait très chaud! Il fait très chaud!
J'enlève ma veste car il fait très chaud.
Il fait très chaud! Il fait très chaud!
J'enlève mon écharpe car
    il fait très chaud.
J'enlève mes gants.
J'enlève mon bonnet.
J'enlève mon chandail.

Let's see what the weather is like today.
Aah! It's so cold! How cold it is!
It's very cold! It's very cold!
I put on my **sweater** because it's
    very cold.
It's very cold! It's very cold!
I put on my **hat** because it's
    very cold.
It's very cold! It's very cold!
I put on my **jacket**.
I put on my **gloves**.
I put on my **scarf**.

Let's go inside now. Aah!
    It is very hot!
It's very hot! It's very hot!
I take off my jacket because it's very hot.
It's very hot! It's very hot!
I take off my scarf because
    it's very hot.
I take off my gloves.
I take off my hat.
I take off my sweater.

Un bonnet

La veste

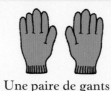

Une paire de gants

Une écharpe

12

La souris et les chaussures

The Mouse and the Shoes

Allez, nous devons partir!
Où sont tes chaussures?
Chaussures, où êtes-vous?
Elles doivent être avec la souris.
Une souris, souris, souris,
est montée dans
    une chaussure marron.
La chaussure a fait tap, tap,
et la souris a roulé, roulé.
Une souris, souris, souris,
est montée dans **une chaussure bleue**.
La chaussure a fait tap, tap,
et la souris a roulé, roulé.
Est montée dans **une chaussure noire**.
Est montée dans
    une chaussure blanche.
Allez, nous devons partir!
Mets tes chaussures. Noue tes lacets.
Oh, non! Voilà la souris!
Cours, cours! La souris arrive!

Come on, we have to go!
Where are your shoes?
Shoes, where are you?
They must be with the mouse.
A mouse, mouse, mouse,
went up
    a **brown shoe**.
The shoe went tap, tap,
and the mouse rolled, rolled.
A mouse, mouse, mouse,
went up a **blue shoe**.
The shoe went tap, tap,
and the mouse rolled, rolled.
Went up a **black shoe**.
Went up
    a **white shoe**.
Come on, we have to go!
Put on your shoes. Tie your shoelaces.
Oh, no! Here comes the mouse!
Run, run! The mouse is coming!

Une chaussure marron

Une chaussure bleue

Une chaussure noire

Une chaussure blanche

Cuisinons!
Let's Cook!

Au supermarché

Nous allons au supermarché.

Veux-tu monter dans **le chariot**?

Voilà la liste.

Nous avons besoin de deux
poivrons verts.

Voilà, un et deux. *Deux poivrons verts.*

Mets-les dans le chariot.

C'est fait.

Maintenant, nous avons besoin de
trois **oignons**.

Voilà, un, deux et trois. *Trois oignons.*

Mets-les dans le chariot.

C'est fait.

Quoi d'autre?

Il nous faut **de l'ail**.

Voilà, une tête d'ail.

Mets-le dans le chariot.

C'est fait.

Maintenant, il nous faut **du pain**.

Voilà, du pain.

Mets-le dans le chariot.

C'est fait.

Du beurre, du yaourt et **des œufs**.

Mets-les dans le chariot.

C'est tout. Allons payer.

Let's Go to the Supermarket

We're going to the supermarket.

Would you like to go in the **cart**?

Here's the list.

We need two
green peppers.

Here, one and two. *Two green peppers.*

Put them in the cart.

It's already there.

Now, we need
three **onions**.

Here, one, two, and three. *Three onions.*

Put them in the cart.

It's already there.

What else?

We need **garlic**.

Here, a head of garlic.

Put it in the cart.

It's already there.

Now, we need **bread**.

Here, bread.

Put it in the cart.

It's already there.

Butter, yogurt, and **eggs**.

Put them in the cart.

That's all. Let's pay.

Un poivron vert

Un oignon

Une tête d'ail

Des œufs

Cuisinons ensemble

Let's Cook Together

Veux-tu m'aider à cuisiner?
Nous allons faire une ratatouille.
   Miam!
D'abord il faut laver les poivrons.
Voilà, lave-les.
Maintenant nous devons les ouvrir.
Enlève **les pépins**. Bien.
Coupe-les en petits morceaux,
   comme ça.
Maintenant lavons **les tomates** et
   les courgettes.
Essuie-les. Bien.
Coupe les tomates avec
   un couteau en plastique.
En petits carrés, comme ça.
Coupe les courgettes en petits carrés.
Et maintenant, faisons-les cuire!
Mets **de l'huile** dans **la poêle**.

Will you help me cook?
We are going to make ratatouille.
   Yummy!
First we need to wash the peppers.
Here, wash them.
Now we have to open them up.
Take out the **seeds**. Good.
Cut them in small pieces,
   like this.
Now let's wash the **tomatoes** and
   the **zucchini**.
Dry them. Good.
Cut the tomatoes with
   a plastic knife.
In little squares, like this.
Cut the zucchini into little squares.
And now, let's fry them!
Put **oil** in the **pan**.

Did You Know?

Ratatouille *is a common dish in southern France. Eggplant, squash, peppers, onions, and tomatoes are sautéed in olive oil. Add salt and pepper and cook.*

Une tomate

Une courgette

Une bouteille d'huile

Une poêle

Le déjeuner

Lunch

C'est l'heure de manger!

Qu'est-ce qu'il y a à déjeuner?

De la soupe et **du poisson**.

Je n'ai pas faim.

Mais tu dois manger un petit peu.

Je n'ai pas faim.

Voilà, la soupe. Goûte-la. Seulement un petit peu.

C'est quoi ce truc orange?

C'est **de la carotte**.

Je n'aime pas les carottes.

Et c'est quoi ce truc vert?

Ce sont **des petits pois**.

Je n'aime pas les petits pois!

C'est quoi ce truc marron?

C'est **de la viande**.

Je n'ai pas faim.

Il y a aussi **de la glace**.

Je veux de la glace! Ça j'aime!

Je croyais que tu n'avais pas faim!

Mange un petit peu de soupe et de poisson et je te donnerai de la glace.

Time to eat!

What's for lunch?

Soup and **fish**.

I'm not hungry.

But you have to eat a little.

I'm not hungry.

Here, the soup. Try it. Only a little bit.

What is this orange stuff?

They're **carrots**.

I don't like carrots.

And what is this green stuff?

They're **peas**.

I don't like peas!

What is this brown stuff?

It's **meat**.

I'm not hungry.

There's also **ice cream**.

I want ice cream! That I like!

I thought you weren't hungry!

Eat a little bit of soup and fish and I'll give you ice cream.

Did You Know?

In France, lunch has always been an important meal. It is a time for good conversation as well as good food. Taking more than an hour for lunch is not unusual. In schools, for example, classes may stop at 11:30 A.M. and reconvene at 1:30 P.M. Some children go home for lunch, and many small shops close during lunchtime so the owners can go home to eat with their families.

Des carottes

Des petits pois

De la viande

De la glace

La soupe folle

Crazy Soup

**La nappe, les bols, les assiettes,
la soupe, la grande cuillère**
—C'est prêt!
C'est l'heure de manger!
Chez mon oncle,
ils mangent la soupe avec **un couteau.**
Qu'est-ce que tu fais?
Manges-tu ta soupe avec un couteau?
Ah, là, là! Tu es fou!
Ah, là, là! Quelle drôle de chose!
Chez Raymond,
ils mangent la soupe avec
une fourchette.
Qu'est-ce que tu fais?
Manges-tu ta soupe avec
une fourchette?
Ah, là, là! Tu es fou!
Ah, là, là! Quelle drôle de chose!
Chez ma sœur,
ils mangent la soupe avec **une cuillère.**
C'est bien! Une cuillère!
Ah, là, là! Comme c'est bon!
Ah, là, là! J'en veux encore un peu!
Encore de la soupe, s'il te plaît!

**Tablecloth, bowls, plates,
soup, big spoon**
—All set!
Time to eat!
In my uncle's house,
they eat soup with a **knife.**
What are you doing?
Do you eat your soup with a knife?
Ay, ay! How crazy you are!
Ay, ay! What a foolish thing!
In Raymond's house,
they eat soup with
a **fork.**
What are you doing?
Do you eat your soup with
a fork?
Ay, ay! How crazy you are!
Ay, ay! What a foolish thing!
In my sister's house,
they eat soup with a **spoon.**
Good thing! A spoon!
Ay, ay! How tasty it is!
Ay, ay! I want a little bit more!
More soup, please!

Une nappe

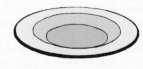

Un bol

Une assiette

Une grande cuillère

L'heure du dîner

Révolution dans la cuisine!

Ah, là, là, que se passe-t-il dans
    la cuisine
pour qu'il y ait une telle révolution?
Le faitout crie et crie
que le dîner est prêt,
et que la table n'est pas mise.
Le plat est arrivé en roulant
pour s'asseoir à table
et il a eu la grande surprise
de voir qu'il n'y avait pas de nappe.
Très effrayé, **le verre** a crié:
Je suis pour l'eau, pas pour la soupe!
La louche, très imbue d'elle-même,
a dit à l'assiette à soupe:
Viens, je vais te servir la soupe
puisque tu n'es pas un verre.
Manger la soupe n'est pas facile si c'est
avec **une fourchette** ou **un couteau**.
Mange la soupe avec **une cuillère**,
ainsi tu ne te saliras pas la figure.
La corbeille à pain très effrayée a crié:
Je me suis salie avec **un cracker**!
Voilà, je viens t'aider!
—a dit **la serviette en papier**.
Silence!—a crié **le sel**—
cette révolution doit cesser;
c'est l'heure de dîner.

Revolution in the Kitchen!

Ay, what happens in
    the kitchen
that there is such a revolution?
The **pot** screams and screams
that dinner is ready,
and the table is not set.
The **dish** arrived rolling
to sit at the table
and it had a big surprise
to see that there was no tablecloth.
Very scared, the **cup** screamed:
I am for water, not for soup!
The **ladle**, very huffy,
told the soup dish:
Come, I will serve you the soup,
since you are not a cup.
Eating soup with a **fork**
and a **knife** is not simple.
Eat soup with a **spoon**,
that way you won't get your face dirty.
Terrified, the **breadbasket** screamed:
I got dirty with a **cracker**!
Here, I will help you!
—said the **napkin**.
Silence!—screamed the **salt**—
this revolution must come to an end;
it is dinnertime.

Un faitout

Un verre

Une corbeille à pain

Un cracker

Le dîner

Dinner

C'est l'heure de dîner!
Le dîner est prêt! Passons à **table**!
Il y a **du rôti**
avec **de la purée de pommes de terre**
    et **de la salade**.
As-tu soif?
Voilà un verre **de lait**.
Bois-le doucement.
As-tu faim?
Voilà un peu **de pain avec du beurre**.
Donne-moi ton assiette, s'il te plaît.
Un morceau de viande, un petit peu
    de purée de pommes de terre,
et un peu de salade.
As-tu besoin d'un couteau pour couper
    la viande?
Tiens, mais fais attention,
    ne te coupe pas.
Si tu termines tout, mais vraiment tout,
je te donnerai **des fraises avec
    de la crème**.

It is dinnertime!
Dinner is ready! Let's sit at the **table**!
There is **roasted meat**
with **mashed potatoes**
        and **salad**.
Are you thirsty?
Here's a glass of **milk**.
Drink it slowly.
Are you hungry?
Here is a little **bread with butter**.
Give me your plate, please.
A piece of meat, a little bit
        of mashed potatoes,
and a little salad.
Do you need a knife to cut
        the meat?
Here, but be careful,
        don't cut yourself.
If you finish it all, and I mean all,
I'll give you **strawberries with
        cream**.

Du rôti

De la purée de pommes
de terre

Une salade

Les fraises avec
de la crème

Dans la cuisine

In the Kitchen

Le dessert

Dessert

Que veux-tu comme **dessert**?

Il y a **des mandarines, des poires, des raisins** et **des bananes**.

Aimerais-tu une mandarine?

Oui, une mandarine.

Épluchons-la.

Enfonce ton ongle.

Comme ça. Regarde comment je fais.

Maintenant, retire **la peau** comme ça.

Sépare **les quartiers**.

*Il y a **des pépins**.*

Retire-les avec ton ongle.

C'est si juteux.

Voilà une serviette en papier.

What do you want for **dessert**?

We have **tangerines, pears, grapes,** and **bananas**.

Would you like a tangerine?

Yes, a tangerine.

Let's peel it.

Stick your nail in.

Like this. Look how I do it.

Now, pull back the **skin** like this.

Separate the **slices**.

*It has **seeds**.*

Take them out with your nail.

It's so juicy.

Here's a napkin.

Did You Know?

Fruit is often eaten at the end of a French meal, and fruit and yogurt are often given to children as dessert. Of course, the fruits offered change with the seasons. Other desserts, such as pastries, are also eaten from time to time. Water and wine are the main drinks served with French meals. After dessert, adults might also have a cup of coffee or an herb infusion, but these are never served during the meal. The coffee is strong and served in small cups (like espresso).

Une mandarine

Une poire

Des raisins

Une banane

Nettoyons la cuisine

Let's Clean the Kitchen

La cuisine est tellement sale!
 Nettoyons-la.
Il faut mettre les assiettes dans
 le lave-vaisselle.
Les assiettes vont en bas.
Les verres vont en haut.
Les couverts vont dans le panier.
Nous devons nettoyer **la table**.
Voilà la lavette. Nettoie la table.
Le sol est tellement sale!
Nettoyons-le.
Tiens, **le balai**.
Balaie le sol.
Voilà **la pelle** pour les saletés.
C'est encore sale.
Maintenant, nous devons laver le sol.
Voilà **la serpillère**.
Lave le sol.

The kitchen is so dirty!
 Let's clean it up.
We need to put the plates in
 the **dishwasher**.
The plates go down here.
The cups go up here.
Silverware goes in the basket.
We have to clean the **table**.
Here's the dishcloth. Clean the table.
The **floor** is so dirty!
Let's clean it.
Here, the **broom**.
Sweep the floor.
Here's the **dustpan** for the trash.
It's still dirty.
Now, we have to mop the floor.
Here's the **mop**.
Mop the floor.

Un lave-vaisselle

Un balai

Une pelle

Une serpillère

L'heure du bain!
Bath Time!

À l'eau, canard!

Duck, to the Water!

C'est l'heure du bain!
La baignoire est remplie
 d'eau chaude.
Laisse-moi t'aider à enlever tes
 vêtements.
Un, deux et trois. Prêt!
À l'eau canard! Couac, couac, couac.
Ne me mouille pas!
C'est l'heure de baigner ce **caneton**.
Ferme tes **yeux**, je vais verser
 de l'eau sur toi.
Un petit peu **de shampooing** pour
 tes cheveux.
Je gratte, gratte, gratte.
N'ouvre pas tes yeux encore.
Les cheveux sont propres.
Avec quoi vais-je laver mon caneton?
Voilà **une éponge** et **un savon**.
Je lave tes **mains**.
Je lave ta petite **figure**.
Je nettoie ton **nez**. Miam! Je l'ai mangé!
Comme mon caneton est propre!
Avec quoi vais-je sécher mon caneton?
Avec cette **serviette** douce, douce.

It's bath time!
The **bathtub** is filled with
 warm water.
Let me help you take off your
 clothes.
One, two, and three. Ready!
Duck, to the water! Quack, quack, quack.
Don't get me wet!
It's time to bathe this **duckling**.
Close your **eyes**, I'm going to pour
 water on you.
A little bit of **shampoo** for
 your hair.
I scratch, scratch, scratch.
Don't open your eyes yet.
Clean hair.
With what do I wash my duckling?
Here is the **sponge** and here is the **soap**.
I wash your **hands**.
I wash your little **face**.
I wash your **nose**. Yum! I ate it!
How clean my duckling is!
What do I dry my duckling with?
With this soft, soft **towel**.

Did You Know?

Bath time is a great opportunity to teach your child the names of body parts. You may want to expand this activity by having your child bathe a doll. Model the behavior and encourage your child to take care of his or her "child" using French words.

La baignoire

Un caneton

Le shampooing

L'éponge

Une serviette, une éponge et du savon

Towel, Sponge, and Soap

Cette chanson est chantée avec
    une serviette, une éponge et du savon.
Nous tirons **le rideau de douche**…
Nous ouvrons **le robinet**…
À l'eau, mon trésor!
Comme ça, comme ça, comme ça,
comme ça je lave mes cheveux.
Comme ça, comme ça, comme ça,
je les ai déjà lavés.
Comme ça, comme ça, comme ça,
comme ça je lave mes mains.
Comme ça, comme ça, comme ça,
je les ai déjà lavées.
Comme ça, comme ça, comme ça,
comme ça je rince ma figure.
Comme ça, comme ça, comme ça,
je l'ai déjà rincée.
Comme ça, comme ça, comme ça,
comme ça j'éclabousse.
Comme ça, comme ça, comme ça.
Oh! J'ai fait une petite flaque.
Sors de l'eau, mon trésor.
Viens et sèche-toi avec cette **serviette**.

This song is sung with
    towel, sponge, and soap.
We open the **shower curtain** . . .
We turn on the **faucet** . . .
Into the water, honey!
Like this, like this, like this,
like this I wash my hair.
Like this, like this, like this,
I already washed it.
Like this, like this, like this,
like this I wash my hands.
Like this, like this, like this,
I already washed them.
Like this, like this, like this,
like this I rinse my face.
Like this, like this, like this,
I already rinsed it.
Like this, like this, like this,
like this I splash water.
Like this, like this, like this.
Oh! I made a little puddle.
Get out of the water, honey.
Come and dry yourself with this **towel**.

Le savon

Le rideau de douche

Le robinet

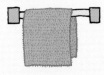

La serviette

Bonne nuit!

Good Night!

Au lit!

Allons dans ta **chambre**.
Trouvons **un pyjama** propre.
Mais d'abord
    un sous-vêtement propre.
Tiens, mets ce sous-vêtement.
D'abord un pied et puis l'autre pied.
Tiens, mets ce pyjama.
D'abord la tête, puis les bras.
Maintenant **le pantalon**.
D'abord une jambe et puis l'autre.
Va dans la salle de bains et brosse-toi
    les dents.
Brosse-les bien, en haut et en bas.
As-tu fait pipi? Non?
Fais pipi alors.
Fais-moi un bisou pour la nuit
et va au **lit**.
Prends ton **nounours** et grimpe
    dans ton lit.
Je vais te couvrir.
Nous allons lire cette **histoire**.
Il était une fois une lune
qui ne voulait pas dormir…

Let's Go to Bed!

Let's go to your **bedroom**.
Let's find clean **pajamas**.
But first
    clean **underpants**.
Here, put on these underpants.
First one foot and then the other foot.
Here, put on these pajamas.
First your head, then your arms.
Now the **pants**.
First one leg and then the other.
Go to the bathroom and brush your
    teeth.
Brush them well, up and down.
Have you made pee pee? No?
Make pee pee then.
Give me good-night kisses
and go to **bed**.
Take your **teddy bear** and get
    in bed.
Now I'll cover you.
We're going to read this **story**.
Once upon a time there was a moon
that didn't want to sleep . . .

Did You Know?

Reading foreign language books to your child three or more times a week is an excellent way to help him or her understand and develop new vocabulary. At first, choose picture books that use repetition, rhyme, and limited vocabulary. Then use the words and expressions learned in real-life conversation.

Une chambre

Un pyjama

Un sous-vêtement

Le lit

La lune

The Moon

La lune, la lune
sortit pour une promenade,
par une belle nuit claire
avec sa nouvelle robe.
Elle se regarda dans un étang.
Elle vit qu'elle était belle.
Elle peignit ses lèvres
en rose.
Cette nuit-là, elle invita une étoile
à se promener,
mais l'étoile lui dit:
Seulement si c'est en voiture.
Elle invita le soleil,
mais le soleil ne voulut pas,
car il ne pouvait
sortir que le jour.
La lune, la lune,
seule et s'ennuyant,
mit son pyjama
et s'endormit.

The moon, the moon
went out for a walk,
on a clear night
with her new dress on.
She looked at herself in a pond.
She saw she was beautiful.
She painted her lips
with the color pink.
That night, she invited a star
to go out for a walk,
but the star told her:
Only if it is by car.
She invited the sun,
but the sun didn't want to,
because he could only
come out during the day.
The moon, the moon,
alone and bored,
put on her pajamas
and fell asleep.

La lune

La nuit

Une étoile

Le soleil

L'heure de jouer!
Playtime!

À cache-cache

Jouons à cache-cache.
Je vais cacher ton petit chien.
Tu fermes les yeux et tu comptes.
*Un, deux, trois, quatre, cinq, six, sept,
    huit, neuf et dix.*
Ouvre les yeux!
Cherchons le petit chien.
Petit chien, où es-tu?
Où es-tu, petit chien?
"Ouaf, ouaf". Je l'entends!
Serait-il derrière **le rideau**?
Non, il n'est pas là.
Serait-il sous **la table**?
Non, il n'est pas là.
Serait-il derrière **le canapé**?
Non, il n'est pas là.
Je sais! Serait-il dans **le tiroir**?
Oui, il est là!
Maintenant tu te caches et je compte.

Hide-and-Seek

Let's play hide-and-seek.
I'm going to hide your doggy.
You close your eyes and count.
*One, two, three, four, five, six, seven,
    eight, nine, and ten.*
Open your eyes!
Let's look for the doggy.
Doggy, where are you?
Where are you, doggy?
"Bow wow, bow wow." I hear him!
Could he be behind the **curtain**?
No, he's not here.
Could he be under the **table**?
No, he's not here.
Maybe he's behind the **sofa**?
No, he's not here.
I know! Will he be inside the **drawer**?
Yes, he is here!
Now you hide and I will count.

Did You Know?

*There are more bilingual than monolingual people in the world.
A popular belief in monolingual countries is that the brain can
only deal with one language, but research has shown that this is not
the case. Quite the contrary, learning languages helps exercise
the brain and build thinking and cultural flexibility. The quality
of the education received is the key to success in any language.*

Un rideau

Une table

Un canapé

Un tiroir

Rangeons

Let's Put It Away

Note: Repeat the *refrain*/chorus after every other object that needs to be put away.

Refrain:
Nous allons ranger.
Quel désordre!
Nous allons ranger ta
   chambre maintenant.
Nous allons ranger.
Quel désordre!
Nous allons ranger ta chambre.

Ouah! Quel désordre!
Nous allons ranger.
*Où vont **les poupées**?*
Les poupées vont sur le lit.
***Les soldats**?*
Les soldats dans la boîte. *(Refrain)*
***Les camions**?*
Nous devons garer les camions.
***La nourriture**?*
La nourriture va dans la cuisine. *(Refrain)*
***Les costumes**?*
Les costumes dans la penderie.
***Le râteau**?*
Que fait le râteau ici?

Chorus:
We're going to put things away.
What a mess!
We're going to clean your
   room now.
We're going to put things away.
What a mess!
We're going to clean your bedroom.

Yikes! What a mess!
We are going to put things away.
*Where do the **dolls** go?*
The dolls go on the bed.
*The **soldiers**?*
The soldiers in the box. *(Chorus)*
*The **trucks**?*
The trucks we have to park.
*The **food**?*
The food goes in the kitchen. *(Chorus)*
*The **costumes**?*
The costumes in the closet.
*The **rake**?*
What is the rake doing here?

Les poupées

Les soldats

De la nourriture

Les costumes

Jouons aux pompiers!

Let's Be Firemen!

Jouons aux pompiers

L'alarme sonne! L'alarme sonne!
Dépêche-toi! Dépêche-toi!
Maintenant, descendons **la perche**.
Mets ta **combinaison**.
Mets tes **bottes**.
Et maintenant ton **casque**.
Monte dans le camion. *Prêt?*
Dégagez la route! *Dégagez la route!*
Déclenche **la sirène**.
Éteignons ce **feu**!
Prends **le tuyau**.
Envoie **l'eau**.
Monte! Monte à l'échelle!
Plus d'eau! *Plus d'eau!*
Excellent travail!
Le feu est éteint.

Playing Firemen

The alarm is ringing! The alarm is ringing!
Hurry! Hurry!
Now, let's go down the **pole**.
Put on your **suit**.
Put on your **boots**.
And now your **helmet**.
Get in the truck. *Ready?*
Clear the way! *Clear the way!*
Turn on the **siren**.
Let's put out the **fire**!
Grab the **hose**.
Blast the **water**.
Up! Climb up the ladder!
More water! *More water!*
Great job!
The **fire** is out.

Did You Know?

You can make a fire truck with a large box. Use big paper plates for the wheels and small ones for the headlights and the siren. Make a hose with a vacuum-cleaner hose or a piece of water hose. Your child can wear a big bowl as a helmet, snow boots, and a big yellow or red shirt for the uniform.

Un pompier

Un casque de pompier

Un tuyau

Un jet d'eau

Le camion de pompiers

The Fire Truck

Dépêche-toi! *Dépêche-toi!*
Allons-y! Allons-y maintenant!
Allons-y! Allons-y maintenant!
Dans **le camion**.
Dans le camion.
Dépêche-toi! *Dépêche-toi!*
Ding, ding, ding, ding.
Ding, ding, ding, ding.
Dépêche-toi! *Dépêche-toi!*
Monte à **l'échelle**!
Monte à l'échelle!
Dépêche-toi! *Dépêche-toi!*
Éteins **le feu**!
Éteins le feu!
Avec beaucoup **d'eau**.
Avec beaucoup d'eau.
Dépêche-toi! *Dépêche-toi!*

Hurry! *Hurry!*
Let's go! Let's go now!
Let's go! Let's go now!
In the **fire truck**.
In the fire truck.
Hurry! *Hurry!*
Ding, ding, ding, ding.
Ding, ding, ding, ding.
Hurry! *Hurry!*
Climb up the **ladder**!
Climb up the ladder!
Hurry! *Hurry!*
Put out the **fire**!
Put out the fire!
With a lot of **water**.
With a lot of water.
Hurry! *Hurry!*

Un feu de maison

Le camion de pompiers

L'échelle

Le feu

Les princesses

Aimerais-tu être Blanche-Neige
   ou Cendrillon?
D'accord. Mets cette **couronne**.
Maintenant, nous avons besoin
   d'un chevalier.
Tu es le chevalier, d'accord?
Utilise le balai comme **cheval**.
Utilise la règle comme **épée**.
Le canapé est **le château**.
Monte sur le canapé.
Chevalier, sauve-nous!
Nous sommes prises au piège dans
   la tour!
Regarde, Cendrillon!
Là, je vois un chevalier.
Crions!
Ici, ici, chevalier!
Il nous a vues! Il nous a vues!
Regarde! Il a une épée! Il va
   nous sauver.

Princesses

Would you like to be Snow White
   or Cinderella?
Okay. Put on this **crown**.
Now, we need
   a **knight**.
You are the knight, okay?
Use the broom as a **horse**.
Use the ruler as a **sword**.
The sofa is the **castle**.
Get on the sofa.
Knight, save us!
We are trapped in
   the **tower**!
Look, Cinderella!
There, I see a knight.
Let's scream!
Here, here, knight!
He has seen us! He has seen us!
Look! He has a sword! He will
   save us.

Did You Know?

*Long ago, France was a country of knights, castles, kings, queens, princes, and
princesses. If you go to France, you will be able to visit magnificent castles all over
the country, and especially along the Loire River. Be sure to visit also the palace of
Versailles in the Paris area and the Louvre Museum in Paris, which was originally
the castle of numerous kings and queens.*

Une princesse

Une couronne

Un chevalier

Une épée

Les pirates

Pirates

Je suis **le pirate** Barbe-Bleue.	I am the **pirate** Blue Beard.
J'ai **la carte du trésor** caché.	Here I have the hidden **treasure map**.
Le trésor est sur **une île déserte**.	The treasure is on a **deserted island**.
Regarde la carte.	Look at the map.
Voilà **le vaisseau**. Tous à bord!	Here is the **ship**. All aboard!
En avant! Allons-y!	Get moving! Quickly!
Je suis **le capitaine**	I am the **captain**
parce que j'ai le chapeau le plus grand.	because I have the biggest hat.
En avant! Allons-y!	Get moving! Let's go!
Commence à ramer, **la tempête** arrive.	Start rowing, the **storm** is coming.
*Nous avons oublié de lever **l'ancre**.*	*We forgot to pull up the **anchor**.*
Quel vent! Aux voiles!	What a wind! To the sails!
La Princesse Belle pleure	*Princess Belle is crying*
car elle est effrayée.	*because she's scared.*
Elle veut un câlin et un bisou,	*She wants a hug and a kiss,*
mais les pirates ne font pas de bisous.	*but pirates don't give kisses.*
D'accord, allez viens et rame.	Okay, then come on and row.
Nous allons dans la mauvaise direction.	*We are going in the wrong direction.*
Tourne.	Let's turn around.
Terre! Terre!	*Land! Land!*
Je vois l'île!	*I see the island!*

Une carte

Un trésor

Les rames

L'ancre

Dans la voiture
In the Car

Au garage

La voiture ne marche pas.
Pouvez-vous m'aider?
Réparons-la.
Elle fait un drôle de bruit au démarrage.
Écoutez: "Rrrrr poufff!"
Quel bruit étrange!
Regardons le moteur.
Passez-moi la clef anglaise,
    s'il vous plaît.
C'est bon.
Passez-moi le marteau.
C'est bon.
Passez-moi le tournevis.
Ça n'est pas ça non plus.
Passez-moi les pinces.
Oh! Et qu'est-ce que c'est?
Je vais tirer. C'est un câble qui a lâché.
Appliquons le plan deux.
Appelons un vrai mécanicien.

At the Auto Mechanic

The car doesn't work.
Will you help me?
Let's fix it.
It makes a funny noise when it starts.
Listen: "Rrrrr puff!"
What a strange noise!
Let's look at the engine.
Pass me the monkey wrench,
    please.
This is fine.
Pass me the hammer.
This is fine.
Pass me the screwdriver.
This isn't it either.
Pass me the pliers.
Oh! And what is this?
I'm going to pull. It's a loose cable.
Now for plan two.
Let's call a real mechanic.

Did You Know?

Living in another country is like driving a car for the first time. The language is the key to the car, but you also need to know what to do with it. If you don't, chances are you will be stuck in the driver's seat with no idea of what to do next. You'll experience culture shock. A good language program offers both language and culture.

Une clef anglaise

Un marteau

Un tournevis

Les pinces

À la station-service

At the Gas Station

Jouons à **la station-service**.
Mets ta **casquette**.
Le plein de super, s'il vous plaît.
***Carte* ou *liquide*?**
Carte. Voilà.
*Ouvrez **le réservoir**, s'il vous plaît.*
Le tuyau est trop court.
Déplacez la voiture.
C'est bon, merci.
Nettoyons la voiture maintenant.
Remonte **les vitres**.
J'apporte **le seau** et **les éponges**.
Essuie bien **les roues**. Avec plus
    de savon.
Enlève **la poussière** à l'intérieur.
Prends ce **chiffon**.
Essuie bien **le volant**.
Maintenant passe **l'aspirateur**
    sur les sièges.
Rinçons la voiture.
Et maintenant séchons-la.

Let's play **gas station**.
Put on your **cap**.
Fill 'er up with super, please.
***Credit card* or *cash*?**
Credit card. Here.
*Open the **tank**, please.*
The **hose** doesn't reach.
Move the car up.
That's enough, thanks.
Now let's clean the car.
Roll up the **windows**.
I'll bring the **bucket** and the **sponges**.
Wipe the **wheels** well. With more
    soap.
Clean the **dust** inside.
Take this **cloth**.
Wipe the **steering wheel** well.
Now run the **vacuum cleaner**
    over the seats.
Let's rinse the car.
And now let's wipe it dry.

Une carte de crédit

De l'argent liquide

Une vitre de voiture

Un volant

Jouons au football

Joue au **football** avec
tes amis David et Sonia!
Nous avons besoin **d'un ballon** et
   d'un filet.
*David est **le gardien de but**.*
*Marquons **un but**.*
Allez, cours, fais une passe.
But! Buuuut!
Maintenant, tu es le gardien de but.
Va au filet.
Allez, Sonia, fais une passe!
Touche!
*Fais **un tir en corner**.*
Frappe avec ta tête.
Allez, cours, fais une passe.
Marquons un autre but!

Playing Soccer

Let's play **soccer** with
your friends David and Sonia!
We need a **ball** and
   a **net**.
*David is the **goalie**.*
*Let's score a **goal** on him.*
Come on, run, pass the ball.
Goal! Goooooooal!
Now, you are the goalie.
Go to the net.
Come on, Sonia, pass the ball!
Out of bounds!
*Make a **corner kick**.*
Hit it with your head.
Come on, run, pass the ball.
Let's score another goal!

Did You Know?

Jump rope is still a very popular game among girls in France. You can play alone or in a group. It is best to start with the two rope turners moving the rope from side to side while a third child jumps. The rope can also be moved in a whole circle.

Un ballon de football

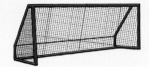

Le filet

Le gardien de but

Touche!

Jouons à la corde à sauter

Let's Jump Rope

Sautons à **la corde**.
C'est ton tour. Un, deux et trois…
Le prénom de Marie
a cinq lettres,
M, A, R, I, E:
Ma-rie.
Le prénom de Camille a sept lettres,
C, A, M, I, L, L, E:
Ca-mil-le.
Maintenant **l'alphabet**.
A, B, C, D, E, F, G, H, I,
J, K, L, M, N, O, P,
Q, R, S, T, U, V, W, X, Y, Z.
Maintenant **les voyelles**.
A, E, I, O, U
A… **amour**
E… **écho**
I… **indien**
O… **ours**
U… **une**

Let's **jump rope**.
It's your turn. One, two, and three . . .
Marie's name
has five letters,
M, A, R, I, E:
Ma-rie.
Camille's name has seven letters,
C, A, M, I, L, L, E:
Ca-mil-le.
Now the **alphabet**.
A, B, C, D, E, F, G, H, I,
J, K, L, M, N, O, P,
Q, R, S, T, U, V, W, X, Y, Z.
Now the **vowels**.
A, E, I, O, U
A . . . **love**
E . . . **echo**
I . . . **Indian**
O . . .**bear**
U . . . **one**

Une corde à sauter

Un indien

Un ours

Un

En promenade
Going Places

Je vais faire du vélo

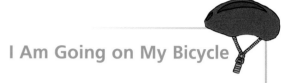

I Am Going on My Bicycle

Nous allons faire du vélo.
Mets ton **casque**—on y va!
Nous allons dans **le parc**.
Il y a plein de gens.
Roulons doucement.
Je fais du vélo. Je fais du vélo.
Je fais du vélo dans le parc.
Nous allons sur **la route**.
Allons vite.
Je fais du vélo. Je fais du vélo.
Je fais du vélo sur la route.
Nous allons dans **la campagne**.
Il y a tellement de bosses!
Je fais du vélo. Je fais du vélo.
Je fais du vélo dans la campagne.
Nous allons grimper la **montagne**.
Montons.
Je fais du vélo. Je fais du vélo.
Je monte avec mon vélo.
Et maintenant je descends!

We are going to ride our bikes.
Put on your **helmet**—and we go!
We are going through the **park**.
There are lots of people.
Let's go slowly.
I'm riding my bike. I'm riding my bike.
I'm riding my bike through the park.
We are going on the **road**.
Let's go quickly.
I'm riding my bike. I'm riding my bike.
I'm riding my bike on the road.
We are going through the **countryside**.
There are so many bumps!
I'm riding my bike. I'm riding my bike.
I'm riding my bike through the countryside.
We are going up the **mountain**.
Let's go uphill.
I'm riding my bike. I'm riding my bike.
I'm riding my bike uphill.
And now downhill!

Did You Know?

This is a great game to play indoors. Sit on the floor and start "pedaling." Jump up and down when hitting a "bump," stick your tongue out and pretend to be out of breath when "going uphill," and scream when "going downhill." You can make a "traffic light" with cardboard and green, yellow, and red cellophane paper. Use a flashlight to simulate turning the lights on and off.

Un casque

Une route

La campagne

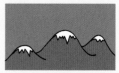

La montagne

Le feu tricolore

The Traffic Light

Rentre dans **la voiture**.
Attache ta **ceinture** et—on y va!
Regarde **le feu**.
Feu vert! Feu vert!
Qu'est-ce que je fais?
Je vais vite, vite, vite.
Biiip, biiip! Tuutt, tuutt!
Feu orange! Feu orange!
Qu'est-ce que je fais?
Je vais doucement, doucement,
    très doucement.
Feu rouge! Feu rouge!
Qu'est-ce que je fais?
Je m'arrête.

Get in the **car**.
Buckle your **belt**—and let's go!
Look at the **traffic light**.
Green light! Green light!
What do I do?
I go fast, fast, fast.
Beep, beep! Honk, honk!
Yellow light! Yellow light!
What do I do?
I go slowly, slowly,
    very slowly.
Red light! Red light!
What do I do?
I stop.

Une voiture

Le feu vert

Le feu orange

Le feu rouge

Allons au parc!

Let's Go to the Park!

Au parc

Nous sommes arrivés au **parc**.
Aimerais-tu aller sur **le toboggan**?
Allez, monte.
Un, deux, trois, quatre, cinq, six.
Très bien, assieds-toi maintenant.
Tiens-toi bien et descends!
Aimerais-tu aller aux **barres**?
Allez, monte.
Un, deux, trois, quatre, cinq, six.
Aimerais-tu aller dans **la tour**?
Allez, monte.
Un, deux, trois, quatre, cinq, six.

In the Park

We have arrived at the **park**.
Would you like to go on the **slide**?
Come on, go up.
One, two, three, four, five, six.
Very good, sit down now.
Hold on tight and go down!
Would you like to go to the **monkey bars**?
Come on, go up.
One, two, three, four, five, six.
Would you like to go to the **tower**?
Come on, go up.
One, two, three, four, five, six.

Did You Know?

Le goûter is snack time in France. A snack is usually eaten by children after school between 4:30 and 5:00 P.M. This snack is generally some bread with butter and chocolate or cookies. Children drink hot chocolate, milk, or fruit juice. Le goûter is important in France because children are hungry when they leave school and dinnertime is far away.

Un parc

Un toboggan

Les barres

Une tour

À la balançoire

On the Swings

Allons à **la balançoire**.	Let's go to the **swings**.
Veux-tu que je te pousse?	Shall I push you?
Et voilà!	There you go!
Plus fort!	*Harder!*
Pourquoi ne pousses-tu pas toi-même?	Why don't you push yourself?
Voyons, soulève tes jambes.	Let's see, pump your legs forward.
Maintenant abaisse tes jambes.	Now pump your legs back.
Comme ça, en avant, en arrière.	Like that, forward, back.
En avant, en arrière.	*Forward, back.*
Veux-tu arrêter?	Do you want to stop?
Allons à **la bascule**.	Let's go to the **seesaw**.
C'est occupé. Nous allons attendre.	It's full. We'll have to wait.
As-tu faim?	Are you hungry?
Oui, je t'ai apporté	Yes, I brought you
un sandwich au jambon.	a **ham sandwich**.

Une balançoire

Une bascule

Un sandwich

Le jambon

Allons nous amuser!

Let's Go to Fun Places!

Au zoo

Nous sommes au **zoo**. Nous sommes au zoo.

Je vois les lions. Nous sommes au zoo.

Le lion fait, "Grrrr".

Le lion dort.

La lionne est là-bas.

Le lion a **une crinière** et la lionne n'en a pas.

Les girafes sont là-bas.

Comme elles ont un grand **cou**!

Leurs **jambes** sont très longues, aussi.

Les éléphants sont là-bas.

Comme ils ont de grandes **oreilles**!

Regarde comment ils attrapent les cacahuètes avec leur **trompe**.

*Regarde, **les tigres**.*

Comme ils ont une grande **gueule**!

Regarde, **les ours**!

Ils sont très grands.

Regarde, voilà les **serpents**.

Les serpents font, "Ssss".

Ils sont très longs.

At the Zoo

We are in the **zoo**. We are in the zoo.

I see the lions. We are in the zoo.

The lion says, "Grrrrr."

The **lion** is sleeping.

The **lioness** is over there.

The lion has a **mane** and the lioness doesn't.

*The **giraffes** are over there.*

What long **necks** they have!

Their **legs** are very long, too.

*The **elephants** are over there.*

What big **ears** they have!

Look how they get the peanuts with their **trunk**.

*Look, the **tigers**.*

What large **mouths** they have!

Look, the **bears**!

They are very big.

Look, here are the **snakes**.

The snakes say, "Ssss."

They are very long.

Did You Know?

French is spoken not only in France, but in many other places as well: in Belgium, Switzerland, Monaco, Canada, in more than twenty African countries, in Martinique, Guadeloupe, Haiti, French Guyana, and Polynesia. From one region to another, there are different accents and vocabulary, but French-speakers always manage to understand one another.

Un lion et une lionne

Une girafe

Un éléphant

Un tigre

Au parc d'attractions

At the Amusement Park

Allons acheter **les billets**.

À quel manège veux-tu aller?

*À **la grande roue**.*

Asseyons-nous. Assieds-toi là.

Donne le ticket à la dame.

Ouah! Comme c'est haut!

Aimerais-tu aller au **carrousel**?

Je te mets sur **le cheval**. Hop!

Tiens-toi bien. Comme ça.

Je vais te tenir, ne t'inquiète pas.

Donne le ticket au monsieur.

Où aimerais-tu aller maintenant?

*Aux **autos-tamponneuses**.*

Cours, allons dans la voiture rouge.
   Monte.

Je viens avec toi, ne t'inquiète pas.

Tu conduis.

*Aux **montagnes russes**.*

Nous ferons cela quand tu seras
   plus grand!

Let's buy the **tickets**.

Which ride do you want to go on?

*On the **Ferris wheel**.*

Let's sit down. Sit here.

Give the ticket to the lady.

Wow! How high!

Would you like to go on the **merry-go-round**?

I'll get you up on the **horse**. Up!

Hold on tight. Like this.

I will hold you, don't worry.

Give the ticket to the man.

Where would you like to go now?

*To the **bumper cars**.*

Run, let's go to the red car.
   Get in.

I'll go with you, don't worry.

You drive.

*The **roller coaster**.*

We'll do that when you are
   older!

La grande roue

Un carrousel

Les autos-
tamponneuses

Les montagnes
russes

Allons au musée!

Let's Go to the Museum!

Au musée de sciences naturelles

Viens, je crois que **les dinosaures**
sont dans cette salle.
*C'est **un tyrannosaure**.*
C'est immense!
Les tyrannosaures mangeaient
les autres dinosaures.
Ils étaient **carnivores**.
Ils avaient **des dents** très pointues.
Regarde, **une empreinte de pied de brachiosaure**.
C'est gigantesque!
Les brachiosaures étaient énormes,
mais ils mangeaient
des feuilles d'arbres.
Ils étaient **herbivores**.
Regarde, c'est un **stégosaure**.
Les stégosaures avaient
une très petite tête.

In the Museum of Natural Science

Come, I think the **dinosaurs**
are in this room.
*It's a **tyrannosaurus**.*
It's huge!
Tyrannosauruses ate
other dinosaurs.
They were **carnivores**.
They had very sharp **teeth**.
Look, a **brachiosaurus footprint**.
It's gigantic!
Brachiosauruses were enormous,
but they ate
tree leaves.
They were **herbivores**.
Look, it's a **stegosaurus**.
Stegosauruses had
very small heads.

Did You Know?

Located in the heart of Paris, the Musée d'Histoire Naturelle is a wonderful place for adults and children to visit. Walking through the dinosaur gallery is a great way to get an idea of what life was like in prehistoric times. After your visit to the dinosaur gallery, you can also take a walk through the Jardin des Plantes, where you will find exhibits of living spiders and snakes!

Un tyrannosaure

Une empreinte de pied

Un brachiosaure

Un stégosaure

Mets un tablier.

Que vas-tu peindre?

Mets un peu de peinture sur la palette.

Au musée d'art

At the Art Museum

Allons voir la salle Dali.
Dali était un peintre espagnol.
*Regarde ce **tableau**.*
Il y a trois visages cachés.
Peux-tu les voir?
Regarde attentivement.
    Vois-tu les visages?
Il y a un enfant, une jeune personne
et une personne âgée.
"Les Trois Ages".
Viens par là.
C'est **une sculpture** de
    Fernando Botero,
un sculpteur et **peintre** colombien.
Regarde, ils ont un atelier de peinture.
Prends **un pinceau**.
Mets **un tablier**.
    Attends, je vais t'attacher.
Maintenant **les peintures**.
Laquelle veux-tu?
Que vas-tu peindre?
Mets un peu de peinture sur **la palette**.
Maintenant touche la peinture
    avec le pinceau.

Let's go to see Dali's hall.
Dali was a Spanish artist.
*Look at this **painting**.*
There are three hidden faces.
Can you see them?
Look closely.
    Do you see the faces?
They are a child, a young person,
and an old person.
"The Three Ages."
Come this way.
This is a **sculpture** by
    Fernando Botero,
a Colombian sculptor and **painter**.
Look, they have a painting workshop.
Get a **brush**.
Put on a **robe**.
    Wait, I'll tie you.
Now the **paints**.
Which ones do you want?
What are you going to paint?
Put a little bit of paint on the **palette**.
Now touch the paint
    with the brush.

Un tableau

Une sculpture

Un pinceau

Une palette

Visite à la famille
Visiting Family

On va chez Grand-père et Grand-mère

Going to Grandma and Grandpa's

Nous allons chez **Grand-mère et Grand-père**.
C'est leur **anniversaire de mariage**.
Nous allons manger **des crêpes**.
C'est délicieux!
Tante Simone et **Oncle** Antoine seront là,
et également ta **cousine** préférée Isabelle.
Mais tu devras jouer aussi avec ton **cousin** Jean.
Nous sommes arrivés! Sors de la voiture.
Salue tout le monde.
Donne un baiser à ta grand-mère et fais-lui un câlin.
Joyeux anniversaire de mariage!

We are going to **grandma and grandpa's** house.
It's their **anniversary**.
We are going to eat **crêpes**.
How delicious!
Aunt Simone and **Uncle** Antoine will be there,
and also your favorite **cousin**, Isabel.
But you will have to play with your **cousin** Jean as well.
We arrived! Get out of the car.
Greet everybody.
Give your grandma a kiss and a hug.
Happy anniversary!

Did You Know?

Crêpes are a kind of paper-thin pancake, very well known and much appreciated in France. They are made with wheat flour or sometimes with buckwheat flour (dinner crêpes), eggs, and milk. After cooking, dessert crêpes can be topped with sugar, fruit, chocolate, or any number of other choices. Dinner crêpes can be topped with anything from ham, cheese, and eggs to seafood. Crêpes are enjoyed throughout France, but they are the specialty of La Bretagne, *which is located in the northwest part of France.*

Le grand-père et la grand-mère

L'oncle et la tante

Les cousins

Le père et la mère

Ma famille

My Family

J'ai **une grand-mère**
dont le nom est Joséphine.
Quand elle **est contente**,
elle passe son temps dans la cuisine.
J'ai **un grand-père**
dont le nom est Étienne.
Quand il **est fâché**,
il passe son temps dans le jardin.
J'ai **une tante**
dont le nom est Nicole.
Quand elle **est fatiguée**,
elle passe son temps dans la maison.
J'ai **un oncle**
dont le nom est Joseph.
Quand il **est triste**,
il passe son temps au café.
J'ai **une sœur**
dont le nom est Suzanne.
Quand elle **s'ennuie**,
elle passe son temps près de la fenêtre.
Oh, ah! Et j'ai aussi
mon **père** et ma **mère**.

I have a **grandmother**
whose name is Josephine.
When she **is happy**,
she spends her time in the kitchen.
I have a **grandfather**
whose name is Steve.
When he **is angry**,
he spends his time in the garden.
I have an **aunt**
whose name is Nicole.
When she **is tired**,
she spends her time in the house.
I have an **uncle**
whose name is Joseph.
When he **is sad**,
he spends his time in the coffee shop.
I have a **sister**
whose name is Susan.
When she **is bored**,
she spends her time at the window.
Uh, oh! And I also have
my **father** and my **mother**.

Je suis content/e.

Je suis fatigué/e.

Je suis triste.

Je m'ennuie.

Les animaux
Animals

Les animaux jouent The Animals Play

Les petits oiseaux qui volent dans l'air
volent, volent, volent, volent, volent.
Les petits poissons qui nagent
    dans l'eau
nagent, nagent, nagent, nagent, nagent.
Les uns et les autres sous le soleil,
les uns et les autres jouent comme moi.
Les petits chevaux qui galopent dans
    la montagne
galopent, galopent, galopent, galopent,
    galopent.
Les petits lapins qui sautent dans
    le champ
sautent, sautent, sautent, sautent,
    sautent.
Les uns et les autres sous le soleil,
les uns et les autres jouent comme moi.
Les petits serpents qui rampent sur
    le sol
rampent, rampent, rampent, rampent,
    rampent.
Les petits écureuils qui grimpent
    aux arbres
grimpent, grimpent, grimpent,
    grimpent, grimpent.
Les uns et les autres sous le soleil,
les uns et les autres jouent comme moi.

The **little birds** that fly in the air
fly, fly, fly, fly, fly.
The **little fish** that swim
    in the water
swim, swim, swim, swim, swim.
These and those under the sun,
these and those play like me.
The **little horses** that gallop in
    the mountains
gallop, gallop, gallop, gallop,
    gallop.
The **little rabbits** that jump in
    the field
jump, jump, jump, jump,
    jump.
These and those under the sun,
these and those play like me.
The **little snakes** that slither on
    the ground
slither, slither, slither, slither,
    slither.
The **little squirrels** that climb in
    the trees
climb, climb, climb,
climb, climb.
These and those under the sun,
these and those play like me.

Un oiseau

Un poisson

Un lapin

Un écureuil

À la ferme

At the Farm

Nous sommes arrivés à **la ferme**.
Voilà **les poules**.
Les poules font, "Cot, cot, cot".
Voilà **les dindes**.
Les dindes font, "Glou, glou, glou".
Regarde, **le coq** est monté sur le toit.
Le coq fait, "Cocorico!"
Aimerais-tu jeter des miettes aux
    poussins?
Les poussins font: "Puiii, puiii, puiiii".
Allons voir **les chevaux**.
Le poulain est avec sa mère,
    la jument.
Le cheval est le père.
Tu veux voir **les vaches**?
Le taureau est le père,
la vache est la mère
et **le veau** est le bébé.
Regarde, le petit veau est
    en train de têter.
Il boit du lait de sa maman.

We have arrived at the **farm**.
Here are the **hens**.
The hens say, "Cluck, cluck, cluck."
Here are the **turkeys**.
The turkeys say, "Gobble, gobble, gobble."
Look, the **rooster** is up on the roof.
The rooster says, "Cock-a-doodle-doo!"
Would you like to throw crumbs to the
    chicks?
The chicks say, "Peep, peep, peep."
Let's go see the **horses**.
The **foal** is with his mom,
    the **mare**.
The **stallion** is the dad.
You want to see the **cows**?
The **bull** is the dad,
the **cow** is the mom,
and the **calf** is the baby.
Look, the little calf is
    nursing.
He's drinking milk from his mom.

Une ferme

Une poule

Un cheval

Une vache

Je ne me sens pas bien
I Don't Feel Well

Chez le docteur

To the Doctor's

Oh! Quelle **toux**!	Oh! What a **cough**!
Dis-moi, où as-tu mal?	Tell me, what hurts?
Est-ce que tu as mal à **la gorge**?	Does your **throat** hurt?
Ouvre grand ta bouche, plus grand.	Open your mouth wide, wider.
Fais ahhhhhh très fort.	Say ahhhhhh very loud.
Très bien!	Very good!
Ta gorge est enflammée.	Your throat is inflamed.
Est-ce que tu as mal aux oreilles?	Do your ears hurt?
Laisse-moi voir cette **oreille**.	Let me see this **ear**.
Cette oreille va bien. Regardons celle-là.	This ear is okay. Let's see this one.
Celle-ci est infectée!	This one is infected!
Quel **nez congestionné**!	What a **runny nose**!
Tiens, **un mouchoir**.	Here, a **tissue**.
Mouche ton **nez**.	Blow your **nose**.
Quel **rhume** tu as!	What a **cold** you have!
Mets **le thermomètre**.	Put in the **thermometer**.
Tu as de **la fièvre**.	You have a **fever**.
Prends **une cuillère à soupe** de ce **sirop**	Take a **tablespoon** of this **syrup**
deux fois par jour.	two times a day.
Bois beaucoup d'eau.	Drink a lot of water.
Reviens dans une semaine.	Come back in a week.
Porte-toi mieux!	Get well!

Did You Know?

Different languages reflect different cultures and different ways of understanding daily life. That is why literal translations can sometimes be linguistically correct but culturally entirely inappropriate. Learning a language is very useful but it is very important to know the culture as well.

Une gorge enflammée

Une oreille

Un nez congestionné

Un nez rouge

Le rhume

Tôt ce matin,
le garçon s'est réveillé,
avec un **mal de gorge**
et une grosse toux.
Euf, euf, euf, euf.
Aïe! Pauvre petit garçon!
Quel rhume il a!
Il a éternué à nouveau.
Atchoum, atchoum, atchoum!
Ses **yeux** larmoient,
son nez le démange.
Sa mère lui apporte
un sirop gris.
Atchoum, atchoum, atchoum!
Aïe! Pauvre petit garçon!
Quel rhume il a!
Il a éternué à nouveau.
Atchoum, atchoum,
    atchoum!

The Cold

Early this morning,
the boy got up,
with a **sore throat**
and a big cough.
Cough, cough, cough, cough.
Ay! Poor little boy!
What a cold he has!
He sneezed again.
Achoo, achoo, achoo!
His **eyes** are watering,
his nose is itchy.
His mother brings him
a gray syrup.
Achoo, achoo, achoo!
Ay! Poor little boy!
What a cold he has!
He sneezed again.
Achoo, achoo,
    achoo!

Un thermomètre

Une cuillère à soupe
de sirop

Le sirop

Les yeux larmoyants

Joyeux anniversaire!

Happy Birthday!

La fête d'anniversaire

The Birthday Party

Quel âge as-tu?

How old are you?

Six ans? Tu es un adulte.

Six? You are a grown-up.

Donne-moi ton oreille. Un, deux, trois, quatre,

Give me your ear. One, two, three, four,

cinq et six.

five, and six.

Et quel âge as-tu?

And how old are you?

Sept ans et demi?

Seven-and-a-half?

Tu es si vieux!

You are so old!

Prends tes **cadeaux**. Ouvre-les.

Take your **gifts**. Open them.

Allez, ouvre-les!

Come on, open them!

*C'est **un hélicoptère**!*

*It's a **helicopter**!*

Et celui-là aussi! Ouvre-le.

And this too! Open it.

Voyons. Qu'est-ce que c'est?

Let's see. What is it?

*C'est **un bateau de pirates**.*

*It's a **pirate boat**.*

Les enfants! Le gâteau!

Kids! The cake!

Did You Know?

The French word for birthday is anniversaire. *In English, the word* anniversary *is used for the celebration of marriage anniversaries. It is easy to understand how these terms are related, since their root refers to once a year. The term for a wedding anniversary in French is more precise. It is* anniversaire de mariage.

Un cadeau

Un hélicoptère

Un bateau

Un pirate

Le gâteau

Le gâteau arrive! Le gâteau!
Le gâteau arrive!
Venez tous!
Asseyez-vous ici.
Les lumières!
Éteignez les lumières, s'il vous plaît!
Chantons. Un, deux et trois.
Joyeux anniversaire,
joyeux anniversaire,
nous te souhaitons tous
un joyeux anniversaire.
Fais **un vœu**.
Souffle **les bougies**.
Souffle plus fort.
Bien! Qui veut du gâteau?
En veux-tu? Oui?
C'est un gâteau au chocolat!
Aimerais-tu **un gros** ou
un petit morceau?

The Cake

The **cake** is coming! Cake!
The cake is coming!
Everybody, come!
Sit here.
Lights!
Turn off the lights, please!
Let's sing. One, two, and three.
Happy birthday to you,
happy birthday to you,
we all wish you
a happy birthday.
Make a **wish**.
Blow out the **candles**.
Blow harder.
Good! Who wants cake?
Do you want some? Yes?
It's a chocolate cake!
Would you like a **big** or
small piece?

Un gâteau

Les bougies

Un gros morceau
de gâteau

Un petit morceau
de gâteau

Allons à la plage!

Let's Go to the Beach!

À la plage

Le **sable** est brûlant!
N'enlève pas tes **sandales**.
Prends **la serviette** dans ton **sac à dos**.
Étends-la sur le sable.
Viens, je vais te mettre
    un peu de **crème solaire**.
Je ne veux pas que tu attrapes
    des coups de soleil.
Un petit peu sur ton visage.
Maintenant sur tes bras et sur tes
    jambes.
Les petits doigts de pied.
Attends! Ne t'en va pas. Viens là!
Mets ta **casquette**, le soleil tape
    très fort.
Aide-moi à faire un trou pour
    le parasol.
Est-ce que je peux emprunter ta pelle?
Je creuse, je creuse, je creuse.
Et maintenant, à l'eau!
Mets ta **bouée**.

At the Beach

The **sand** is hot!
Don't take off your **sandals**.
Take the **towel** from your **backpack**.
Spread it on the sand.
Come here, I'll put
    some **sunscreen** on you.
I don't want you to get
    burned.
A little bit on your face.
Now on your arms and on your
    legs.
Your little toes.
Wait! Don't go away. Come here!
Put on your **cap**, the sun is
    very strong.
Help me make a hole for
    the **umbrella**.
Can I borrow your shovel?
I am digging, digging, digging.
And now, to the water!
Put on your **inner tube**.

Did You Know?

You can set up a "beach" in the playroom or the backyard. Make a sun with construction paper. Mark off a pretend swimming area with tape. You can make a sandbox with a large container filled with sand and toys. Use a beach bag with beach towels, sand toys, and sunscreen. Have fun!

Les sandales

La crème solaire

Le parasol

La bouée

Les châteaux de sable

Sand Castles

Faisons **un château de sable**.	Let's make a **sand castle**.
Voilà **le seau**.	Here is the **bucket**.
Voilà **la pelle**.	Here is the **shovel**.
Remplis le seau avec du sable.	Fill the bucket with sand.
Maintenant renverse-le.	Now flip it over.
Tapote doucement.	Pat it softly.
Pain dur, se ramollit.	*Hard bread, soften up.*
Pain dur, se ramollit.	*Hard bread, soften up.*
Pain dur, se ramollit.	*Hard bread, soften up.*
Maintenant soulève le seau. Doucement!	Now lift the bucket. Slowly!
Comme c'est beau!	*How beautiful!*
Choisis **un moule** pour construire la tour.	Choose a **mold** to build a tower.
Remplis-le avec du sable.	Fill it with sand.
Renverse-le très doucement.	Flip it very slowly.
Prends **le rateau** et fais un chemin.	Take the **rake** and make a path.
Maintenant ramollis-le avec la main.	Now smooth it with your hand.
Prends la pelle et creuse **un fossé**.	Take the shovel and dig a **moat**.
Ne jette pas de sable!	Don't throw sand!
Regarde! Là tu as **des coquillages** et **des cailloux**	Look! Here you have **shells** and **stones**
pour décorer le château.	to decorate the castle.
Quel beau château!	*What a beautiful castle!*

Un château de sable

Un seau

La pelle

Un rateau

Au printemps
In the Spring

Mouvements du printemps

Spring's Movements

L'escargot, l'escargot
avance très lentement.
Avance lentement comme un escargot.
Le papillon, le papillon
volète parmi les fleurs.
Volète parmi les fleurs comme
    le papillon.
La grenouille, la grenouille
saute dans l'eau.
Saute dans l'eau comme la grenouille.
La coccinelle, la coccinelle
est très petite.
Tu es petit/e comme la coccinelle.
Le vent, le vent
souffle et souffle.
Souffle comme le vent.
La fleur, la fleur
ondule dans le vent.
Ondule comme la fleur.
Le printemps est là!

The snail, the snail
moves very slowly.
Move slowly like the snail.
The butterfly, the butterfly
flutters among the flowers.
Flutter among the flowers like
    the butterfly.
The frog, the frog
jumps in the water.
Jump in the water like the frog.
The ladybug, the ladybug
is very small.
You are small like the ladybug.
The wind, the wind
blows and blows.
Blow like the wind.
The flower, the flower
waves in the wind.
Wave like a flower.
Spring is here!

Did You Know?

"Il pleut bergère" is a classic French song for young children. In the past, families would choose a little boy or girl who would be in charge of caring for the sheep on the farm. Though this tradition doesn't exist anymore, the song is still sung and enjoyed by children and their parents as well.

Un escargot

Un papillon

Une grenouille

Une coccinelle

La pluie

The Rain

Il pleut! Mets tes **bottes**.
Maintenant **l'imperméable**.
Ouvrons **les parapluies**.
Quelle pluie! C'est **une averse**!
 Chantons!
Il pleut, il pleut, bergère,
Presse tes blancs moutons.
Allons à ma chaumière,
Bergère, vite allons.
J'entends sur le feuillage
l'eau qui tombe à grand bruit.
Voici, venir l'orage.
Voici, l'éclair qui luit.
Sautons dans **la flaque d'eau**!
La pluie s'est arrêtée. *Ça sent si bon!*
C'est l'odeur du printemps.

It's raining! Put on your **boots**.
Now the **raincoat**.
Let's open the **umbrellas**.
What a rain! It's a **downpour**!
 Let's sing!
It's raining, it's raining, shepherdess,
Hurry along your white sheep.
Come to my cottage,
Shepherdess, let's go quickly now.
I hear the sound of the heavy
rain falling on the leaves.
See, the storm is coming.
See, the lightning is lurking.
Let's jump in the **puddle**!
It stopped raining. *It smells so good!*
It's the smell of spring.

Les bottes

L'imperméable

Le parapluie

Une averse

En été
In the Summer

Allons pêcher

Chuuut! Silence!
Nous allons voir s'il y a du poisson.
Jette du pain. Comme ça, plus de
    miettes.
Il y a beaucoup de poissons.
Prends ta **canne à pêche**.
Accroche **l'appât** à **l'hameçon**.
Lance ta **ligne**. Très bien.
Attendons.
Quelque chose a mordu!
Tiens bien ta canne et tire. Tire!
*C'est **une botte**. Beurk!*
Mets plus **d'appât** et lance la ligne.
Quelque chose a mordu!
Tiens bien ta canne et tire. Tire!
*Ouah! C'est **un poisson géant**.*
Ça doit être **le roi des poissons**.
Mets-le dans **le panier**.
Mets plus d'appât et lance ta ligne.
Quelque chose a mordu!
C'est une boîte de conserve. Beurk!
Au moins c'est **une boîte de sardines**!

Let's Go Fishing

Shhhh! Silence!
We are going to see if there are fish.
Throw bread. Like this, more
    crumbs.
There are many fish.
Take your **fishing pole**.
Put the **bait** on the **hook**.
Cast the **line**. Great.
Let's wait.
Something bit!
Hold your pole tight and pull. Pull!
*It's a **boot**. Yikes!*
Put on more **bait** and cast the line.
Something bit!
Hold your pole tight and pull. Pull!
*Wow! It's a **giant fish**.*
It must be the **king of fish**.
Put it in the **basket**.
Put on more bait and cast the line.
Something bit!
It's a can. Yikes!
At least it's a **can of sardines**!

Did You Know?

Throw a blue tablecloth on the floor and use a large box or a coffee table placed upside down as a boat. For the fishing activity, place a few objects in the "river" and try to fish them out with a pole made with a stick and cord. (You may want to attach magnets to the pole and the objects you're fishing for.) Show a picture or a puppet of a wave, crocodile, and waterfall for the song.

Une canne à pêche

Un hameçon

Un poisson géant

Une boîte de sardines

Sur la rivière

By the River

Note: After each verse, repeat the *refrain*/chorus.

Refrain:
Dans mon **bateau** je rame.
Sur la rivière je vais,
sur la rivière je vais, sur la rivière je vais.

Une vague géante arrive!
Une vague arrive! Une vague arrive!
Couvre ton nez!
Une vague arrive là.
Bonne nouvelle elle s'en va. *(Refrain)*

Un crocodile arrive!
Rame vite, rame vite!
Un crocodile arrive! Un crocodile arrive!
Un crocodile arrive là.
Bonne nouvelle il s'en va. *(Refrain)*

Une cascade arrive!
Qu'allons-nous faire, qu'allons-nous
    faire?
Une cascade arrive!
Une cascade arrive là.
Bonne nouvelle elle s'en va. *(Refrain)*

Chorus:
In my **boat** I row.
By the river I go,
by the river I go, by the river I go.

A huge **wave** is coming!
The wave is coming! The wave is coming!
Cover your nose!
A wave is coming here.
Good thing it's going away. *(Chorus)*

A **crocodile** is coming!
Row fast, row fast!
A crocodile is coming! A crocodile is coming!
A crocodile is coming here.
Good thing it's going away. *(Chorus)*

A **waterfall** is coming!
What do we do, what do we
    do?
A waterfall is coming!
A waterfall is coming here.
Good thing it's going away. *(Chorus)*

Un bateau

Une vague

Un crocodile

Une cascade

En automne
In the Fall

Les squelettes

The Skeletons

Note: After each hour, repeat the *refrain*/chorus "Tomb, tomb, tomba-la-ca-tomb, tomb, tomb, tomba-la-ca-tomb."

Quand **l'horloge** sonne une heure,
les squelettes sortent de leurs tombes.
Quand l'horloge sonne deux heures,
Les squelettes regardent **l'horloge**.
Quand l'horloge sonne trois heures, les
squelettes touchent leurs **pieds**.
Quand l'horloge sonne quatre heures, les
squelettes cirent leurs **chaussures**.
Quand l'horloge sonne cinq heures, les
squelettes font **du tricycle**.
Quand l'horloge sonne six heures, les
squelettes prennent **le train**.
Quand l'horloge sonne sept heures, les
squelettes font de **la trottinette**.
Quand l'horloge sonne huit heures, les
squelettes montent à **moto**.
Quand l'horloge sonne neuf heures, les
squelettes **ne bougent pas**.
Quand l'horloge sonne dix heures, les
squelettes **ne peuvent être vus**.
Quand l'horloge sonne onze heures, les
squelettes **ne peuvent être
entendus**.
Quand l'horloge sonne douze heures, les
squelettes ronflent dans **la nuit**.

When the **clock** strikes one,
the **skeletons** get out of their tombs.
When the clock strikes two,
the skeletons look at the **clock**.
When the clock strikes three, the
skeletons touch their **feet**.
When the clock strikes four, the
skeletons polish their **shoes**.
When the clock strikes five, the
skeletons ride their **tricycles**.
When the clock strikes six, the
skeletons ride on a **train**.
When the clock strikes seven, the
skeletons ride on **scooters**.
When the clock strikes eight, the
skeletons ride on their **motorcycles**.
When the clock strikes nine, the
skeletons **don't move**.
When the clock strikes ten, the
skeletons **can't be seen**.
When the clock strikes eleven, the
skeletons **can't be
heard**.
When the clock strikes twelve, the
skeletons snore in the **night**.

Un squelette

Un tricycle

Un train

Une trottinette

Fermez bien les yeux!

Cours, attrape-la!

Je t'ai attrapé!

Une méchante sorcière

A Bad Witch

Une vilaine **sorcière** marche
   derrière nous.
Ferme bien les yeux.
Ouvre-les, tu verras!
Cours, cours! Attrape la sorcière!
Bravo! Tu l'as attrapée!
Un vilain **magicien** marche derrière nous.
Ferme bien les yeux.
Ouvre-les, tu verras!
Cours, cours! Attrape le magicien!
Bravo! Tu l'as attrapé!
Un vilain **fantôme** marche derrière nous.
Ferme bien les yeux.
Ouvre-les, tu verras!
Cours, cours! Attrape le fantôme!
Bravo! Tu l'as attrapé!
Un vilain **monstre** marche derrière nous.
Ferme bien les yeux.
Ouvre-les, tu verras!
Cours, cours! Attrape le monstre!
Bravo! Tu l'as attrapé!

A bad **witch** is walking
   behind us.
Close your eyes tight.
Open them, you'll see!
Run, run! Catch the witch!
Great! You caught her!
A bad **wizard** is walking behind us.
Close your eyes tight.
Open them, you'll see!
Run, run! Catch the wizard!
Great! You caught him!
A bad **ghost** is walking behind us.
Close your eyes tight.
Open them, you'll see!
Run, run! Catch the ghost!
Great! You caught him!
A bad **monster** is walking behind us.
Close your eyes tight.
Open them, you'll see!
Run, run! Catch the monster!
Great! You caught him!

Une moto

Une sorcière

Un fantôme

Un monstre

En hiver

In the Winter

La tempête de neige

The Snowstorm

Il fait très froid.	It is very cold.
Oh! Comme il fait froid!	*Oh! How cold it is!*
Si f-f-f-roid!	How c-c-c-old!
J'ai très froid.	I am very cold.
Et toi? As-tu froid?	What about you? Are you cold?
J'ai très froid.	*I am very cold.*
Regarde, il neige.	Look, it is snowing.
Comme c'est beau!	*How beautiful!*
Il neige! *Merveilleux!*	It is snowing! *Great!*
Touche **la neige**.	Touch the **snow**.
Comme la neige est froide!	How cold is the snow!
Ouh! Comme c'est froid!	*Uy! How cold it is!*
Si f-f-f-roid!	How c-c-c-old!
Faisons **des boules de neige**.	Let's make some **snowballs**.
Prends un peu de neige. *Comme ça.*	Get some snow. *Like this.*
Fais une boule. *Comme ça.*	Make a ball. *Like this.*
Un, deux, trois…	One, two, three . . .
Lance-la!	Throw it!
Aïe!	Hey!
Je t'ai eu!	Got you!

Did You Know?

In the winter months, the French love to ski. Often, they go skiing in Les Alpes, mountains located in the southeast of France and in the bordering countries of Switzerland and Italy, or in Le Jura, the natural border between France and Switzerland, or even in Les Pyrénées, which separate France from Spain.

Une tempête de neige

Une grosse boule

Une boule moyenne

Une petite boule

Le bonhomme de neige

The Snowman

Note: Repeat the *refrain*/chorus after each verse.

Refrain:
Je suis **un bonhomme de neige**
et je danse mieux en hiver.

Une grosse boule!
Une boule moyenne!
Et une petite boule!
Pour la tête. *(Refrain)*

Je bouge *mes* **bras** comme ça!
Je bouge *mes* **pieds** comme ça!
Je bouge *mon* **chapeau** comme ça!
Un, deux, trois. *(Refrain)*

Oh, non! Le soleil est apparu!
Il fait si chaud, si chaud, si chaud!
Je fonds! Je fonds!
Je suis **une petite flaque d'eau**.
Éclabousse-moi: splatch, splatch,
   splatch. *(Refrain)*

Chorus:
I am a **snowman**
and I dance better in winter.

*A **big ball**!*
*A **medium-sized ball**!*
*And a **small ball**!*
For the head. *(Chorus)*

I move *my* **arms** like this!
I move *my* **feet** like this!
I move *my* **hat** like this!
One, two, three. *(Chorus)*

Oh, no! The sun came out!
It is so hot, so hot, so hot!
I am melting! I am melting!
I am a **little puddle of water**.
Splash in me: splash, splash,
   splash. *(Chorus)*

Les bras

Les pieds

Un chapeau

Une flaque d'eau

J'utilise la technologie
I Use Technology

Mettons des photos sur Facebook

Let's Post Pictures on Facebook

Mettons des **photos** sur **Facebook**.
Celles de mon anniversaire?
Oui, tu peux choisir **tes dix préférées**.
Cherchons-les.
Quelles photos est-ce que tu aimes?
J'aime celle où je fais tomber le gâteau.
D'accord, et celle avec
  ton bulldozer?
Oui! Et celle-ci aussi.
Nous en avons dix maintenant.
Mettons-les dans **un album**.
Regarde! **Grand-mère** a posté
  un commentaire.
Laisse-moi le lire.
«J'adore cet avion!
Qui te l'a offert?»
*Maman, dis-lui que c'est Jean qui me l'a
  offert. C'est mon meilleur, meilleur,
  meilleur ami dans le monde entier.*
Oh, **grand-père** a écrit lui aussi!
Il dit qu'il veut jouer avec ton
  bulldozer.
*Bien sûr! Dis-lui que je vais jouer
  avec lui.*

Let's post **pictures** on **Facebook**.
The ones from my birthday?
Yes, you can choose **your ten favorites**.
Let's look for them.
What pictures do you like?
I like the one where I dropped the cake.
Okay, and what about the one with
  your bulldozer?
Yes! And this one too.
We have ten now.
Let's put them in **an album**.
Look! **Grandma** posted
  a comment.
Let me read it.
"I love that airplane!
Who gave you that?"
*Mom, say that Jack gave it to me.
  He's my best, best,
  best friend in the whole world.*
Oh, **Grandpa** also wrote!
He says that he wants to play with your
  bulldozer.
*Sure! Tell him that I'll play
  with him.*

Une photo

Un bulldozer

Facebook

Allumer

Nous parlons avec les cousins

We Talk with Our Cousins

Tu veux parler avec **les cousins**?
Oui!
Alors passe-moi **l'ordinateur portable**.
Je vais l'allumer.
*Bonjour, **tante** Lucy! Où es-tu?*
Au parc.
Tu veux parler avec tes cousins?
Oui, oui. Je veux parler avec Monique.
Bonjour, Monique! Qu'est-ce que tu fais?
*Je parle avec toi **sur Skype**.*
C'est pas vrai! Et quoi d'autre?
*J'essaie **mon nouveau vélo**. Tu veux
    le voir?*
Oui, approche l'ordinateur.
*Oh, mais le mien est **plus grand**!*
Je ne t'entends pas!
N'appuie pas sur ce bouton!
Oh non! Nous avons perdu la connexion!
    Nous essaierons **plus tard**.
Argh!
Pendant ce temps, nous pouvons jouer
    avec **l'iPod**.

Do you want to talk with **your cousins**?
Sure!
Then pass me **the laptop**.
*I'll **turn it on**.*
*Hello, **Aunt** Lucy! Where are you?*
At the park.
Do you want to talk with your cousins?
Yes, yes. I want to talk with Monica.
Hi, Monica! What are you doing?
*I'm talking with you **on Skype**.*
No kidding! And what else?
*I'm riding **my new bike**. Do you want to
    see it?*
Yes, bring the computer closer.
*Oh, but mine is **bigger**!*
I don't hear you!
Don't touch that button!
Oh no! We've lost the connection!
    We'll try again **later**.
Agh!
Meanwhile, we can play
    with the **iPod**.

L'ordinateur portable

Les cousins

La tante

iPod

En ville
In the City

Nouvel An à Chinatown

New Year's in Chinatown

Papa, qu'est-ce que c'est?
C'est un défilé de **dragons**.
Tu veux y aller?
Oui, je veux le voir!
Tiens-moi bien la main.
Il y a trop de **monde**.
*C'est quoi ce **bruit**?*
Des personnes qui **jouent du tambour**
    pour la Danse du Dragon.
Et là-bas, ce sont **les lions**.
Et qu'est-ce qu'ils font?
Ils fêtent le Nouvel An Chinois.
Quand j'étais un petit garçon en Chine,
    tes grands-parents me donnaient
    toujours **une enveloppe rouge**
    pour le Nouvel An.
Et qu'est-ce qu'il y avait dedans?
De **l'argent**.
Cela porte **chance** pour la
    nouvelle année.

Dad, what's that?
It's a **dragon** parade.
Do you want to go there?
Yes, I want to see it!
Hold my hand tight.
There are too many **people**.
*What's that **noise**?*
People playing the **drums**
    for the Dragon Dance.
And those over there are the **lions**.
And what are they doing?
They are celebrating Chinese New Year.
When I was a little boy in China, **Grandma**
    and Grandpa always gave me
    a red envelope for the
    New Year.
And what was inside the envelope?
Money.
It brings **good luck** for the
    New Year.

Did You Know?

When children learn a new language, they develop academic, intercultural, and language-learning abilities that will serve them well no matter what the future brings in terms of studies, jobs, business opportunities, personal interests, or travel. There is no crystal ball that can predict which language will be most useful for your child in the future. Not to worry! Learning a new language trains your brain to learn languages in general.

Un dragon

Un tambour

Une enveloppe rouge

Argent

Manger en ville

Eating in the City

J'ai faim. Je veux manger maintenant!

Oui. Allons voir les stands de nourriture. Il y a de la nourriture chinoise, de la pizza, des **hamburgers** et des hot-dogs, des sandwichs...

Qu'est-ce que tu veux?

Je veux **une pizza nature**.

D'accord.

Et qu'est-ce que tu veux **boire**?

Il y a du jus, de **l'eau**, de la limonade, du Coca-Cola...

Du Coca-Cola, s'il te plaît.

Maman, ils ont **les fruits** que tu aimes!

«Salade de kiwis». Miam!

Ça a l'air intéressant.

Je vais en essayer une.

Allons nous asseoir à **cette table**.

Qu'est-ce que vous voulez faire maintenant?

Pourquoi ne montons-nous pas dans **un bus à deux étages**?

Oui, oui, **sur l'étage du haut**!

L'arrêt de bus est là.

Courez, un bus arrive!

I'm hungry. I want to eat now!

Yes. Let's check the food stands. There's Chinese food, pizza, **hamburgers** and hot dogs, sandwiches . . .

What do you want?

I want **plain pizza**.

Okay.

And what do you want **to drink**?

There's juice, **water**, lemonade, Coke . . .

Coke, please.

Mommy, they have the **fruit** that you like!

"Kiwi salad." Mmm!

That seems interesting.

I'll try one.

Let's sit at **that table**.

What do you want to do now?

Why don't we ride **a double-decker bus**?

Yes, yes, **in the upper deck**!

The **bus stop** is there.

Run, a bus is coming!

Eau

Fruits

Un hamburger

Un bus à deux étages

À l'école
At School

Le premier jour d'école

The First Day of School

Bonjour, comment tu t'appelles?
Annie.
Je suis Madame Lebrun.
Bienvenue dans notre classe.
Maintenant que nous sommes tous là, asseyons-nous **en rond**.
Aujourd'hui, nous allons parler de nos choses préférées.
Pouvez-vous deviner ma **couleur** préférée?
Bleu!
Rouge!
Jaune!
Orange!
Non, c'est **violet**!
Maintenant **c'est à vous** de parler de vos **jouets** préférés.
Quel est ton jouet préféré, Jean?
L'iPhone de maman.
Et pourquoi aimes-tu l'iPhone de ta maman?
*Parce que je peux **jouer du piano** et parler à mon papa.*
Et **le tien**, Valérie?
*J'aime mes nouveaux **cubes**.*
Ils sont énormes!

Hello, what's your name?
Annie.
I'm Miss Brown.
Welcome to our classroom.
Now that we're all here, let's sit in **a circle**.
Today, we are going to talk about our favorite things.
Can you guess my favorite **color**?

Blue!
Red!
Yellow!
Orange!
Nope, it's **purple**!
Now **it's your turn** to tell us about your favorite **toys**.
Which is your favorite toy, John?
My mom's iPhone.
And why do you like your mom's iPhone?

*Because I can **play piano** and talk with my daddy.*
And **yours**, Valerie?
*I like my new **blocks**.*
They're huge!

Bleu

Rouge

Jaune

Orange

Faisons les mathématiques!

Let's Do Math!

Bonjour, ma classe!	Good morning, class!
Aujourd'hui, nous allons compter des choses **ensemble**.	Today we are going to count things **together**.
Combien y a-t-il de **filles** dans la classe, Marie?	How many **girls** are in the class, Mary?
Compte pour voir.	Count them and see.
Une, deux, trois, quatre, cinq, six, sept.	*One, two, three, four, five six, seven.*
Très bien, il y a sept filles dans la classe!	Correct, there are seven girls in the class!
Et maintenant, combien y a-t-il de **biscuits** dans **le pot à biscuits**?	And now, how many **cookies** are in the **cookie jar**?
Douze!	*Twelve!*
Trente-sept!	*Thirty-seven!*
Nous allons voir…	**Let's see** . . .
Oh, non! **Zéro!**	Oh, no! **Zero!**
Qui a mangé les biscuits?	Who ate the cookies?
Pas moi!	*Not me!*
Robert… Qu'est-ce que tu as dans les mains?	Bobby . . . what's that in your hands?
Peux-tu nous dire combien de biscuits il y avait dans le pot à biscuits?	Can you tell us how many cookies there were in the cookie jar?
Je ne sais pas.	*I don't know.*

Un *ou* une

Deux

Trois

Quatre

J'adore mes animaux

I Love My Pets

Je veux un chaton

I Want a Kitty

Maman, mon amie Lisa a un nouveau chaton.

J'en veux un, moi aussi!

Mais nous avons déjà un mini-zoo ici. Voyons:

Un chien,

trois **grenouilles,**

deux **hamsters,**

une tortue

et **un lézard.**

*Mais je voudrais avoir **un chat**!*

Et les petits chatons sont si mignons...

Et où le chaton va-t-il dormir?

Dans mon lit.

Et qui va lui donner à manger?

Moi.

Et qui va nettoyer la boîte avec **le caca** et **le pipi**?

Maman, c'est beurk. Je n'aime pas ça. Tu vois?

De toute façon, papa **est allergique aux** chats.

*Eh bien, papa n'a qu'à ne pas entrer dans **ma chambre**!*

Pauvre papa!

Nous ne pouvons pas avoir de chat, mais nous pouvons aller jouer avec celui de Lisa quand tu veux.

D'accord, **allons-y**!

Mommy, my friend Lisa has a new kitty.

I want one too!

But we already have a small zoo here. Let's see:

One dog,

three **frogs,**

two **hamsters,**

one turtle,

and **one lizard.**

*But I'd like to have **a cat**!*

And little kittens are so cute . . .

And where is the kitty going to sleep?

In my bed.

And who is going to feed him?

I will.

And who is going to clean the box with the **poop** and **pee**?

Mommy, that's yucky. I don't like that. See?

Anyway, Daddy **is allergic to** cats.

*Then Daddy doesn't have to go into **my room**!*

Poor Daddy!

We can't have a kitty, but we can go play with Lisa's whenever you want.

Okay, **let's go**!

Un hamster

Une tortue

Un lézard

Un chat

Mon chien va à l'école canine

My Dog Goes to Dog School

Papa, **pourquoi** Max doit-il aller à l'école?

Parce qu'il doit apprendre les maths.

C'est pour rire! Il doit **apprendre** à écouter.

Bonjour! Je suis **le dresseur** de chiens.

Comment s'appelle ton **chien**?

Max.

Bonjour, Max. Voyons voir ce que tu peux faire.

Max, **assis**!

Oh, non, Max! Ne te sauve pas! Tu dois écouter ton dresseur.

Max, marche **avec moi**!

Bon chien, Max!

Je vais jeter **ce bâton**.

Maintenant, Max, va chercher!

Max, **cours vite**! Allez, allez, allez!

Bien! Il l'a attrapé!

Daddy, **why** does Max need to go to school?

Because he needs to learn his math.

I'm just kidding! Because he needs **to learn** how to listen.

Hi! I'm the dog **trainer**.

What's your **dog's** name?

Max.

Hi, Max. Let's see what you can do.

Max, **sit**!

Oh, no, Max! Don't walk away! You have to listen to your trainer.

Max, walk **with me**!

Max, good boy!

I'm going to throw **this stick**.

Now, Max, go fetch!

Max, **run fast**! Go, go, go!

Yay! He got it!

Un chien

Caca

Assis!

Cours!

Nous partons en voyage
We're Going on a Trip

À l'aéroport

At the Airport

Vos **passeports**, s'il vous plaît.	**Passports**, please.
Où allez-vous aujourd'hui?	Where are you traveling today?
À Tunis, en Tunisie.	To Tunis, Tunisia.
Merci.	Thank you.
Voilà vos passeports.	Here are your passports.
Et ces tickets sont pour **les valises**.	And these tickets are for **the suitcases**.
Bon voyage!	Have a good trip!
Enlevez **vos chaussures** et mettez-les dans **le bac**.	Take **your shoes** off and put them in **the tray**.
On va où?	*Where are we going?*
Nous allons **à la porte d'embarquement**.	We're going to **the boarding gate**.
*Je veux aller **aux toilettes.***	*I want to go **to the bathroom**.*
Attends jusqu'à ce que nous trouvions nos places.	**Wait until** we find our seats.
Rangée trente-deux.	**Row** thirty-two.
Voilà nos **places**!	Here are our **seats**!
Ces toilettes sont tout petits, papa!	*This bathroom is tiny, Daddy!*
Notre salle de bains à la maison est beaucoup plus grande que ça.	*Our bathroom at home is much bigger than this.*

Did You Know?

People in many countries in North Africa speak Arabic and French. Tunisia is a strikingly beautiful country with many destinations popular with history and nature fans. Filmmaker George Lucas chose several desert towns in Tunisia to film his Star Wars *saga. These towns and landscapes are very popular with tourists all over the world. An online search will show you pictures for Tataouine, Matmata, the isle of Djerba, Tozeur, and other locations featured in* Star Wars.

Le passeport

Les toilettes/la salle de bains

La place

Les valises

À l'hôtel

At the Hotel

*Nous allons dormir ici **cette nuit**?*

Oui, et demain, nous partirons tôt pour aller à Tamerza.

Est-ce que tu t'es brossé **les dents**?

Oui.

Va au lit alors.

Nous allons partir **tôt**, alors essaie de dormir. Bonne nuit!

Debout!

Il faut se préparer pour prendre **le bus d'excursion**.

Vos billets, s'il vous plaît! Merci.

On est arrivé?

Arrête de demander. Nous sommes presque arrivés.

Regarde! Vois-tu **les murailles**?

Où? Où?

Là-bas, au sommet de **la montagne**!

Nous allons passer deux jours ici et ensuite, nous irons visiter les villes de ***La Guerre des Étoiles***.

Ouiii! Est-ce qu'Anakin sera là?

Je ne sais pas.

Il est peut-être sur une autre **planète**!

---

*Are we going to sleep here **tonight**?*

Yes, and tomorrow we'll leave early to go to Tamerza.

Did you brush your **teeth**?

Yes.

Go to bed then.

We're going to leave **early**, so try to sleep. Good night!

Wake up!

We have to get ready to take **the tour bus**.

Tickets, please! Thank you.

Are we there yet?

Stop asking. We're almost there.

Look! Can you see **the walls**?

Where? Where?

Over there, up on **the mountain**!

We'll spend two days here and then we'll visit the ***Star Wars*** towns.

Yay! Will Anakin be there?

I don't know.

Maybe he's on another **planet**!

Le bus

L'hôtel

La montagne

Les murailles

Jeux
Games

Dans ma maison

Qu'est-ce qu'il y a **dans le garage**?
*Il y a **une voiture**.*
*Il y a **un vélo**.*
*Il y a **un tracteur**.*

Qu'est-ce qui se passe **à l'entrée**?
*Il y a une femme **qui sort** de l'ascenseur.*
*Il y a un monsieur **qui promène** son chien.*
*Il y a un garçon **qui pleure**.*

Que font les gens **dans le gymnase**?
*Une femme **soulève** des poids.*
*Un monsieur **court** sur le tapis.*
*Des enfants **jouent au** basket.*

Que se passe-t-il **dans le salon**?
*Le grand-père **regarde la télé avec** son petit-fils.*
*La grand-mère **lit une histoire à** sa petite-fille.*
*Le bébé **joue avec** son ourson.*

Que font les adultes **dans la cuisine**?
*Le père **essuie** la vaisselle.*
*La mère **fait la cuisine**.*
*La voisine **parle** sans arrêt.*

Que se passe-t-il **dans la salle à manger**?
*Le papa **veut** encore de l'eau.*
*La grand-mère **mange** tous les spaghettis.*
*La maman **est très en colère**.*

Qu'est-ce qu'il y a **dans la chambre**?
*Il y a **un lit** rouge.*
*Il y a **une armoire** pleine de vêtements.*
*Il y a **un bureau** et des livres.*

Que se passe-t-il **dans la salle de bains**?
*La mère **se brosse les cheveux**.*
*Le garçon **se lave les dents**.*
*La petite fille **fait pipi et caca**.*

À quoi jouent les enfants **dans la
  salle de jeux**?
***Les filles** jouent à la poupée.*
***Le grand garçon** joue avec des cubes.*
***Le petit garçon** joue avec son train.*

In My House

What's **in the garage**?
*There's a **car**.*
*There's a **bicycle**.*
*There's a **tractor**.*

What's happening **in the lobby**?
*There's a woman **getting out of** the elevator.*
*There's a man **walking** his dog.*
*There's a boy **crying**.*

What are the people doing **in the gym**?
*A woman **lifts** weights.*
*A man **runs** on the treadmill.*
*Some children **play** basketball.*

What's going on **in the living room**?
*The grandpa **watches TV with** his grandson.*
*The grandma **reads a story to** her granddaughter.*
*The baby **plays with** his teddy bear.*

What are the adults doing **in the kitchen**?
*The father **is drying** the dishes.*
*The mother **is cooking**.*
*The neighbor **is talking** nonstop.*

What's happening **in the dining room**?
*The dad **wants** more water.*
*The grandma **is eating** all the spaghetti.*
*The mom **is very angry**.*

What's **in the bedroom**?
*There's a red **bed**.*
*There's a **closet** full of clothes.*
*There's a **desk** and books.*

What's happening **in the bathroom**?
*The mother **is combing her hair**.*
*The boy **is brushing his teeth**.*
*The little girl **is making pee and poop**.*

What are the children playing **in the
  playroom**?
***The girls** are playing with their dolls.*
***The older boy** is playing with blocks.*
***The little boy** is playing with his train.*

How to Play the Game

This game is designed to be played as the traditional "Tic-Tac-Toe" game ("Force 4" in French). The building in the large image will be your board. The building is divided into three floors with three rooms each, just as the typical 3 × 3 boxes on a "Tic-Tac-Toe" board are. As you play the game, you can get extra vocabulary practice by asking each player to say something about the room before he or she puts a token down. Therefore, it is a good idea to practice the vocabulary *before* playing the game!

Here are several sample questions and answers you can use as prompts to get kids talking about the different scenes in the house.

Jeux
Games

Dans la classe de Mademoiselle Calamité...

Un garçon déguisé en **pirate** saute sur la table. Tu le vois?

Il y a **de nombreux livres** dans la bibliothèque. Combien? [Six]

Il y a **plusieurs chiffres** 4 cachés. Tu les vois?

De quelles couleurs sont **les balançoires**? [Rouge et vert]

À côté de la fille à la perruque rouge, il y a **une poubelle.** Tu la vois?

Mademoiselle C. joue **d'un instrument.** Lequel? [Un trombone]

Il y a deux garçons qui jouent **à cache-cache.** Tu peux les trouver?

Au **chevalet** il y a un enfant qui peint avec les mains. Tu le vois?

Il y a **une addition** sur **le tableau.** Tu la vois?

Il y a **un éléphant en pâte à modeler.** Où est-il? [Sous **une chaise**]

Autres choses que vous pouvez chercher:
Un toboggan
Une balance
Un ordinateur
Une radio
Un iPod
Un carnet
Des craies grasses
Des feutres
Des ciseaux
Un ballon de basket
Un avion
Un cheval

In Miss Calamity's Class . . .

A boy dressed as a **pirate** is jumping on the table. Do you see him?

There are a **number of books** on the bookshelf. How many? [Six]

There are **several number** 4s hidden. Do you see them?

What colors are the **swings**? [Red and green]

Beside the girl with the red wig there is a **trash can.** Do you see it?

Miss C is playing an **instrument.** Which one is it? [A trombone]

There are two boys **playing hide-and-seek.** Can you find them?

At the **easel** there's a boy painting with his hands. Do you see him?

There's an **addition problem** on the **board.** Do you see it?

There's a **play-dough elephant.** Where is it? [Under a **chair**]

Other things you can look for:
A slide
A seesaw
A computer
A radio
An iPod
A notebook
Crayons
Markers
Scissors
A basketball
An airplane
A horse

75

About the Authors

Ana Lomba's breakthrough method "Ana Lomba's Easy Immersion®" is changing the way people think about and interact with young children learning languages. Ana's lively resources and detailed lesson plans are favorites with teachers and parents who want to nurture young children's innate language abilities. A Princeton University graduate, Ana has taught Spanish from preschool to college and held leadership positions with national language organizations in the United States. Ana is a native of Madrid, Spain, and she lives with her husband and three children in Princeton, New Jersey. For more information about Ana's teaching resources, e-storybook collections, and iPad applications, go to www.analomba.com.

Marcela Summerville is the founder of Spanish Workshop for Children, an award-winning Spanish immersion program for young children in Philadelphia. Marcela is also a workshop presenter sharing her innovative teaching methodology at prestigious conferences across North America. In addition, she has published articles on teaching a second language to youth. Marcela is a native of Patagonia, Argentina, and she lives with her husband and two children in Philadelphia. For more information, visit www.spanishworkshopforchildren.com.

Frank D. Jacobs

Pedro Pérez del Solar, a native of Peru, holds a Ph.D. in Spanish Literature and has been a press illustrator since 1990. Pedro is currently an assistant professor of Spanish Literature and Culture at the University of Texas at El Paso.